EMPOWER YOUR CONFIDENCE

SILENCE YOUR INNER CRITIC, FREE UP YOUR MIND FROM OBSESSIVE WORRY AND UNCERTAINTY, AND BE YOUR BEST AT ALL TIMES

SCOTT ALLAN

"When you create a vision of the person you most want to become, you begin to build a new identity, and in this journey of creating your confidence, sense of self-worth, and ability to handle life's challenges are limitless."

SCOTT ALLAN

Empower Your Confidence.

Silence Your Inner Critic, Free Up Your Mind from Obsessive Worry and Uncertainty, and Be Your Best at All Times

MORE BESTSELLING TITLES FROM SCOTT ALLAN

Empower Your Thoughts

Drive Your Destiny

Relaunch Your Life

The Discipline of Masters

Do the Hard Things First

Undefeated

No Punches Pulled

Fail Big

Rejection Free

Built for Stealth

Check out the complete collection of books and training here:

www.scottallanbooks.com

Empower Your
Confidence

Silence Your Inner Critic, Free Up Your Mind from Obsessive Worry and Uncertainty, and Be Your Best at All Times

By Scott Allan

Copyright © 2022 by Scott Allan Publishing all rights reserved.

Empower Your Confidence by Scott Allan

All rights reserved.

No part of this publication may be reproduced, distributed or transmitted in any form or by any means, including photocopying, recording, or other electronic or mechanical methods, without the prior written permission of the publisher, except in the case of brief quotations embodied in critical reviews and certain other noncommercial uses permitted by copyright law.

The resources in this book are provided for informational purposes only and should not be used to replace the specialized training and professional judgment of a health care or mental health care professional.

www.scottallanbooks.com

ISBN (Paperback): 978-1-990484-14-8

ISBN (eBook): 978-1-990484-12-4

ISBN (Hardcover): 978-1-990484-13-1

CONTENTS

Introduction: Empower Your Confidence 11
Part 1: Barriers to Building Self-Confidence 25
Part 2: The Types of Confidence 65
Part 3: Reinventing Your Confidence, Brain and Neuroplasticity 87
Part 4: The Bulletproof Confidence Upgrade 121
Conclusion 166

"Life is not easy for any of us. But what of that? We must have perseverance and above all confidence in ourselves. We must believe that we are gifted for something and that this thing must be attained."

— **Marie Curie**

Introduction: Empower Your Confidence

"Confidence is the ability to feel beautiful without needing someone to tell you." — **Mandy Hale**

The power of a confident mindset is the most valuable asset you can invest your time, energy and focus into. With a confident mind flows a confident posture, a smile, and a confident way of thinking.

Confidence is much more than just a good feeling, but rather, it's a way of being, behaving, and existing. It is a positive, focused energy source directed with initiative into becoming the person you want to be, or, reaching the goals you desire to achieve.

When you begin to think, act and behave with confidence, all your limitations fall to the way side. The impossibilities that once held you back now become fragile walls that you can easily break through because you're certain you can do anything you set out to achieve.

Confidence is your definitive self that embraces your inner lifeforce. Unbreakable confidence is the driving force behind massive action that makes key decisions, fueling your heart and mind with limitless potential.

That said, there are inevitable obstacles that obstruct the journey, making it challenging for you to maintain this level of confidence. The reason this happens is, every new level of confidence you advance towards is matched with a challenge that must be overcome for you to keep crushing it. There is no such thing as "making it" and then you get to coast the rest of the way.

If your life is a steady progression of growth, every level of this growth increases in difficulty. This is how you become so good that nobody can ignore you.

To live a life on your terms and feel truly empowered from within, you need to feel, be and act self-confident. After all, only when you feel truly comfortable in your heart and mind, and embrace who you are, can you feel totally comfortable with yourself in your own skin—without needing external validation or social evidence to tell you so.

Empower Your Confidence: *This Book's Purpose*

The purpose of this book is to train you to be your best at all times, to break your uncertainty, and level up your self-esteem. As you will discover throughout this training, your confidence level has nothing to do with what anyone thinks of you. It has nothing to do with what you have or don't have, and it certainly has nothing to do with your social status, job position or wealth.

People who seemingly have everything can still lack total confidence in their self-worth and abilities.

Your external circumstances can affect your confidence, but in the end, confidence is a mindset that you control. Regardless of what you look like, who you know, where you live, where you went to school, or the size of your bank account, self-confidence begins with this idea:

"I am worthy of everything I choose to be in this moment."

Confidence is a choice, backed up by tiny action steps taken every day. Yes, it really is that simple. But we complicate what self-confidence really is, and more importantly, how to create it. Yes, confidence is a feeling and a reality that you create for yourself. It's not given to you, nor do you have to earn it through validation.

Stop waiting for permission to be confident. Give yourself permission to be who you are and begin to lean hard into the belief that you are capable of limitless potential. You have capabilities, limitless potential and untapped reservoirs of talent and skill yet to be discovered.

Self-confidence comes down to this one simple concept: "It is the relationship you have with yourself. It's how you feel about yourself when you're alone with yourself."

When you are genuinely self-confident:

- You can control how you feel about YOU, and this creates certainty in who you are, your mission, and purpose in life.

- You can break down any barrier standing between you and your dreams.

- You know what you want and, you're willing to do whatever it takes to get there.

- You know that you're not limited by external circumstances or your present skills. You can learn new skills and cultivate a new environment.

That's the kind of confidence you need to excel in this life, and this happens when you Empower Your Confidence.

I know it isn't always easy to be and act confident, especially if you have had a life filled with difficulties. If you've lived a life characterized by adversaries, self-doubt and discouragement are bound to afflict and affect you in many different ways.

But fear not. You're in good hands...your own! Self-confidence is yours to master and build over time. In this book, my intention is to show you exactly how to do that.

Empower Your Confidence: *The Struggle with Self-Esteem*

Self-doubt is more of a dilemma than an actual diagnosable problem.

It creates a miserable situation inside of you—a situation of chaos, hurt, and lack of contentment—that makes you feel like you will never be enough, inadequate, and at times, isolated. A self-doubt affliction can be so bad that sometimes, you can get to a point where you feel 100% sure that you won't ever achieve success, to the point where you stop trying and give up.

Yes, winning is almost impossible when you are in self-doubt, and self-doubt typically happens because of negative, self-limiting thoughts, which in most cases, may not even be your thoughts.

The reality of life is that we don't come into this world with self-doubt, uncertainty or negative thoughts. You pick them from your interaction with people around you as you grow up.

The interrupting, negative thoughts that somehow made their way to your mind come from various avenues. Perhaps your environment was that of extreme criticism, abuse, neglect, and tensions. Maybe you went through some form of bullying in school and college. Perhaps you've had a few challenges to taste, and every time you'd falter, there was a voice around you labeling you incompetent.

The thoughts and beliefs you nurture now developed from scores of ancient beliefs drilled into your subconscious mind from many external sources. Your doubts tell you how you are not adequate, smart, beautiful, good, capable, confident, wonderful, and brilliant enough.

You didn't come into this world with these toxic, negative perceptions; you learned and developed them until they become learned behaviors that are now part of your belief system and psyche.

If your despair is mounting and threatening to pull you under, know now that there is a path to creating emotional freedom. This wasn't ever and will never be the end of the world. I want you to think of this book as your doorway leading into a new world, the next plateau, and a new way of life that you get to create and become your own master.

The truth is that, you have the power to change your thoughts, feelings, and beliefs. Moreover, you can transform them completely. You may find this surprising, but you are in total command of your thoughts, beliefs, emotions, feelings, behaviors, attitudes, and decisions. Nobody else is responsible for these things: only you are!

It is not your partner's responsibility to keep you positive nor your children's' duty to keep you confident. Your boss or manager isn't liable to elevate your mood. Neither is it your parents' responsibility to make you feel strong time and again. They might try to help you with this on the way, but ultimately, you must choose for yourself: "Will I walk through this day with my head up high, or keep it low, staring at the ground?"

You are the only one who can do all these things for yourself because confidence is a personal thing, and only you can empower yourself from within.

When that is clear, it also becomes critical to understand that, no matter how despair-ridden you feel right now, you have to take steps to become more confident and self-assured. You know that you alone can take care of and win over this challenge.

This realization may cause you to start losing your piece of mind; after all, years of not believing in yourself haven't done you any good. They have stripped you of the courage you need to start believing in the person you were born to be, the limitless YOU that is just on the other side of the river....and all that stands between who you are now and the person you desire to become is a decision.

The feeling is scary and overwhelming. You find yourself questioning the idea—and reality—of believing in yourself long-term. Let me reassure you that, as you begin to work on yourself each day, as you push through the obstacles holding standing between you and everything you desire, growth is inevitable. You will start believing in yourself. You will BE confident and empowered, and you will be on your way to greatness. You will become all the great things that you have ever wanted in this lifetime.

But realize this: It's near impossible to be confident all the time in all situations. Thus, there is nothing wrong with being unconfident now and then. However, when you let that become your fate, problems start to crop up in every facet of your life, personal and professional. But from now, all of this is all going to change. You can build a better, confident heart and mind.

My Lifetime Struggle with Confidence

Like I mentioned above, I was once drowning in the muddy pool of self-doubt. It wasn't just me, but my dreams, ambitions, aspirations, and goals were drowning with me, too. But, fortunately, I was aware of the situation and determined to free myself from this affliction.

This inner determination motivated me to start working on the many elements tied to self-confidence, gradually fixing each element, and course-correcting my path one step at a time. The results I experienced were amazing. I couldn't believe that something as simple as believing in myself was helping me feel better and grow bigger in life—by leaps and bounds at that.

But the real pivot started when I took that belief and turned it into a purpose-driven massive action blueprint

Compelled by the positive results I experienced through taking this action, I began applying the same rules in different areas of my life and, started experiencing great results every time. When I shared the strategies with others, they began to experience life-changing rewards.

By that time, I felt convinced that I was on the right track: I was 100% sure that empowering your self-confidence is the only way to living a happy, fulfilling and more meaningful life.

The result that I experienced from empowering this confidence motivated me to write this book and share what I had learned about the power of confidence and how to cultivate it for decades of growth. Like planting the garden, you need to throw your seeds down and get to work.

Empower Your Confidence: About This Book

Empower Your Self-Confidence is not like every other book on confidence. It is more like a guide that will be by your side, constantly educating and supporting you as you take steps to become stronger, confident, happier, and ultimately, build a life of extreme satisfaction and fulfillment.

This guide focuses on helping you build self-confidence, one strategy at a time, and is the one element that is integral to your well-being and prosperity in life.

To truly empower your self-confidence, you must also debunk some myths concerning confidence.

Firstly, you must understand that the path to a confident you begins with setting a clear intention to become more self-confident today than yesterday. And tomorrow, you will make the same decision, to continue the momentum of scaling up as you move through the growth process.

If you don't set a specific and clear intention, you can do everything right without getting the results. In this book, we will focus in on the power of intention, and how you can direct your mental focus for greater intention with every action, moving you closer towards your goals.

The right path that leads to confidence should include taking tangible and purposeful actions. You will face inner resistance while trying to do what you wish to achieve. When that happens, we often mistake our emotions as our true feelings holding us back from danger.

The fear of failure is really the fear of believing in yourself. You may think the universe is giving you a signal to steer clear of that goal because it's "not your destiny." When in fact, the road leading towards your destiny is bound to be filled with fear and scary moments. But when you lead with confidence, you know that you will be just fine.

However, the truth is far from that. In reality, it is years of self-doubt taking its toll on you. All the negativity you have picked up from all around you throughout your life jumps up and begins to eat away at you. It is not the universe conspiring against you. It is your fear keeping you from achieving greatness in every aspect of your life.

Another prevalent myth about confidence is that you cannot always control your self-doubts and fears. Since you've ingrained that negativity into your subconscious from early childhood, you feel incapable of diminishing, controlling, or eradicating it. It sticks with you, like glue to paper.

Consider this: *Do you keep listening to music you don't like, or continue reading a boring book after struggling to get through the first few chapters?*

Just like you have the power to close that book or close your music player application, you have the power to switch off that annoying noise in your head. It is just the noise of your own mind, and you can turn it off—if you are determined enough.

Another prevalent myth related to confidence is that, people often assume it is the perception others have of you. Confidence isn't about what others think of you, nor how they label you. People can judge you all they want, even condemn you as much as they like, but they cannot decide who you are or what you can do. Those are choices only you have control over.

So, your confidence is not about what others think of you or make of you. It is primarily about what you think of yourself. If you ever feel any other way, it's because you've allowed the myth to trap you.

To be specific in what confidence truly is, confidence is the relationship you have with yourself. It is how you spend time with yourself, how you treat yourself, and how you view yourself and the outside world from your lens or worldview. The entire structure of confidence builds on the view you form of yourself, not of anybody else but your identity.

Other factors, experience, thoughts, emotional perception, relationships, social identity, and self-worth do play an important role in your life and confidence. In later parts of this book, we shall discuss all of these factors to ensure you have a clear idea of the steps you need to take to empower your confidence and start living your best life yet!

Empower Your Confidence: The Book Structure

I've divided this book into different sections, with each section teaching specific lessons. The lessons are deliberately small and succinct to ensure you can apply the information easily. The idea is to make every section "enough on its own" so that you can open any part of the book as per your need, read it, and get a profound takeaway from it.

I always value people and their time. I know how precious time is for all of us. Considering that, I've structured the book in a manner where you can read it from the start, middle, or end: absolutely from anywhere you like.

Perhaps you'd like to improve your confidence in your relationships; well then, you dive straight into that chapter and begin learning. Or you want to learn more about building better confidence by beating procrastination; simply jump right to that lesson. You can also check out my book Do the Hard Things First for a deep dive into overcoming procrastination and mastering difficult tasks.

By the time you complete Empower Your Confidence, you will know exactly what's right or wrong in your life. You will know the mistakes you are making and how to correct them, and you will have started taking positive action towards fixing them.

Your life is about to change for the better, a claim I can make with 100% conviction because, when I started applying the various strategies I teach in this book, my life changed for the better. This has led to a life of constant and never-ending growth, and that, my friends, always leads to greatness.

All I ask of you is that you be willing to take action and ready to embrace the change that takes you towards your best life ever!

Now is the time to discover a level of untapped confidence that already exist within you. You just have to know how to find it, and then, once you rediscover this goldmine, feed it like a hungry lion.

See you on the inside…

Scott Allan

"Confidence… thrives on honesty, on honor, on the sacredness of obligations, on faithful protection and on unselfish performance. Without them it cannot live."

Franklin D. Roosevelt

Part 1: Barriers to Building Self-Confidence

"Confidence is the most beautiful thing you can possess."

Sabrina Carpenter

Roadblocks on the Journey to Self-Confidence

Why does confidence elude you? Why can't you just feel confident all the time? What keeps you from believing in yourself?

A barrier is an obstruction that keeps you from pursuing a certain path. These obstructions are both external and internal impediments that hold you back from growing into a more self-assured—and calmer—version of yourself.

These hindrances are big holes in your psyche that make you feel incompetent, inadequate, insecure and fearful. Only when you truly believe something has power over you do you let it take over.

If you are allowing certain blockades to turn your world upside down, it means you have given it the power to do so. It's like handing over the keys of your car to somebody else and saying, "here, you drive this because I can't."

In this particular section of the book, we'll briefly look at each contributing factor together with one strategy to resolve the situation. If you only work on that one strategy with consistency and commitment for the next 30 days, you'll experience a shift in both thought and behavior.

This leads to feeling great about who you are, and prompts you to try harder, to strive for more, and to challenge how far you can truly go. Combine the different solutions taught for each obstacle to build a pack of powerful solutions you can call on whenever you need them. That's how you yield compounding results.

Now, let's dive in and start learning more by working on the different blockades to confidence.

The Legacy of Fear

"Fear is the path to the dark side. Fear leads to anger; anger leads to hate; hate leads to suffering." — **Yoda**

Fear is the root cause of suffering, and the path to suffering is housed in a lack of self-belief.

Being afraid of something means that the particular thing, be it an idea, goal, subject, or person, has created some form of terror in your mind. There is a level of anxiety about it that keeps you from moving forward.

For instance, you may plan to write and publish a book, but you feel scared that it won't sell, and that people may laugh at you for failing to achieve your dream of becoming a published author. Or perhaps you want to apply for a job in a company that you've always wanted to work for. But instead of going for what you want, you apply for the easier jobs because your fear convinces you that you're not good enough for the job you really desire.

If you dig into the fear a little deeper, you might come to realize that you think the book won't sell because you are unsure of your capabilities as a professional writer. Or if you actually do get hired by the company for the position you truly want, you fear not measuring up to their standards and that they could fire you.

If you dissect these two issues separately, the root cause will most likely boil down to a lack of confidence—and self-defeating doubts—about what you're worth to the world.

Just because you don't feel confident enough, you give the fright of unauthentic apprehensions the opportunity to take over your mind. This element of 'dread' guarantees that you won't move forward. You stay stuck in neutral. As a result, you don't follow through with your passion for authoring a book. You let the dream slip beneath the waves of infinity, where all dreams go to die.

You never grow or move close to your desired reality, and slowly, you only have complaints to write of, eventually leading to living a life you never wanted, but a life that you end up building from the ruins of failed action. This leads to regret later on, and living in regret is a painful form of existence.

This reason alone is enough to build a confident mindset. To steer clear of a destiny filled with broken dreams and wishing for one more chance that may never come, you must act now to empower this confident mindset.

For a long time, you may have allowed your fears to control you. These fears have made you dance to their tune for years. Don't you think it is time to turn things around for a change?

Let me share a powerful way to make this a reality for you.

How to Overcome Fear

Dale Carnegie blessed us with one of the most brilliant ways to break and overcome the vicious 'fear' cycle. He said:

"Inaction breeds doubt and fear. Action breeds confidence and courage. If you want to conquer fear, do not sit home and think about it. Go out and get busy."

Fear is a state of mind triggered and built by emotions. When you perceive something as daunting, difficult, challenging, or life-threatening, your brain receives the 'fear' stimulus. The brain then signals the release of hormones that trigger fear, and you start "feeling" scared— or experience other related emotions like anxiousness, overwhelm, or chronic stress.

The less action you take to remedy the situation, the more trepidation takes over you. In such situations, we often become stagnant. For example, if you feel scared of pitching your business to a group of potential investors, you may drop the idea of going to the investors' meeting. Out of fear, you may stay in bed the entire day and may not even work on the simplest of tasks lined up for that day.

When this continues as a regular pattern, it becomes your default habit for dealing with any crisis, no matter how big or small. Your lifestyle becomes a life centered around fear, anxiety, and feelings of low self-worth and shame.

A lifestyle governed by fear is never a healthy or productive one. Hence, the key to breaking this cycle of fear is to get moving, build momentum and charge forward with the fear. You don't wait for the fear to leave; you take it with you on the ride.

Here's what you can do to start this process:

- Think of what you ought to be doing right now.

- Write down that task as clearly as possible. Clarity is key.

- Ask yourself why you aren't taking any action right now. What is triggering your fears?

- Write that down once again.

- Now, only think of one thing you can easily do right now to displace that fear. For example, in the case of attending the investors' meeting, if speaking on a one-on-one level is what scares you, you could send an email to the group and ask to have a virtual meeting instead of a real-time one. Perhaps you could psych yourself up by presenting your pitch to your mirror image.

- Identify one thing you can do right now, and then **do it**. Without thinking twice, just do it. Trust me, if you keep thinking of how, when, what, how, and where to do it, you will only keep thinking and never really get to work. You will think yourself into doing nothing. That isn't what you want right now because that's how you have allowed your fears to interfere with creating the kind of life you really want. You want things to be different. So, you need to do things differently.

- Once you take that one step, see how you feel. Tune into your feelings and take account of the intensity of your fear.

- On a scale of 1 to 10, rate how scared you felt before doing that one task and then after engaging in it. Even if the needle has moved low by a single point, you have a little victory to your credit.

This victory will cement the belief that taking action makes a difference, which will fuel your desire to keep taking action.

Your job now is to take consistent action daily; that way, you will keep combatting and eliminating your fears.

Learned Helplessness

If confidence isn't yet present in your life, it is likely that every time you sit to work, you hear some creepy statements orbiting your mind: "I can't do this! I get bored by the task easily. It is too difficult, or, I am just not cut out for this."

Such statements have often bothered most of us—and when you repeat these statements every minute, you reinforce your beliefs that you will never be able to do anything. We fall into analysis paralysis and freeze up.

The reality of life is that you are not the only one going through a predicament. We are all in this together. That said, what's important right now is to understand how such statements hijack your thoughts, making you feel powerless to stop it.

These statements are examples of learned helplessness, which is a huge roadblock to confidence. Learned helplessness occurs when you stop trying due to consistent failure. This phenomenon is common among people who feel incapable of coping with the different challenges life throws at them.

Imagine you are trying to work on a task that you somehow feel incapable of completing. You feel discouraged, but you decide to give it another go. Unfortunately, failure becomes your fate the second, third, and fourth time. By the time you encounter your fifth letdown, you feel certain you aren't bound to succeed.

Instead of giving yourself the courage to try another time, you keep looking at the disappointments to your credit. You use that narrow lens to see yourself, which is why you never see yourself as capable enough. As a result, your self-esteem starts to plummet, and before you realize it, you lose the confidence to keep moving forward.

Learned helplessness is sabotaging because it causes you to stop trying altogether. It affects your performance in school, work, relationships, personal growth, and every other aspect of your life.

When you see yourself struggling in different areas of your life, you are bound to feel depressed. Learned helplessness is not depression, nor does it necessarily always lead to or cause depression. That said, you cannot deny that learned helplessness causes unhappiness by creating feelings of inferiority.

To let go of these feelings, let's discuss several key strategies for tackling learned helplessness.

How to Manage Learned Helplessness

To manage learned helplessness, it is first important to understand how you constructed this attitude over time. There are three primary ways through which you can manifest learned helplessness:

Negative self-talk. This refers to the habit of negatively talking to yourself at all times. When you only say demeaning things to yourself such as, "I can't do this," "I am a loser," and so on, you start to believe these suggestions.

Believing in such suggestions gives them a chance to burrow into your subconscious mind, where they start influencing your belief system. Gradually, you feel like a lost cause only because that's what you have been telling yourself all this time. What you believe is what you become and soon you're acting out your beliefs until it becomes your identity.

The assumption that you will never grow. This assumption comes from nurturing a fixed mindset. Carol Dweck, a renowned Stanford Professor, has conducted years of research that have revealed the existence of two kinds of mindset: fixed and growth mindsets.

The former suggests you have limited growth and learning capacity; thus, you can only do things to a certain extent. On the other hand, the latter suggests that hard work, practice, and consistency can help you bring about any change and success because growth never stops, and you can accomplish whatever you want in life.

When you nurture a fixed mindset, you stop growing and feel stagnant. That's when learned helplessness steeps into your life and schemes a plan towards lack of confidence. In contrast, by nurturing a growth mindset, you can easily find your long-lost confidence and find the will to keep growing and moving forward in life.

Displaying a negative view of different changeable circumstances. Life never remains the same. Change is the only constant thing in all our lives. This is a law of the universe and you can never overrule it. When something is a fact, it is best to accept it as it is and work towards moving forward. Since accepting change is difficult, when a certain change enters your life, you become resistant to it and perceive it negatively.

Instead of doing your best to adapt to it, you constantly fight it and display a negative view of it. That's how learned helplessness becomes a constant in your life.

Let us discuss how you can work on this particular area to weaken the attitude and default habit of learned helplessness.

How to Overcome Learned Helplessness

As mentioned, assuming you will never grow is a fixed mindset belief. The only way to get rid of it is by nurturing a growth mindset. That may seem like a daunting task to you right now, but if you stay calm and approach it pragmatically, you will realize that it isn't as challenging a job as you may believe it is.

Cultivating a growth mindset means you continuously choose to focus on growing bigger, better and stronger. To achieve a goal, you don't stay stagnant or follow the same old practices you've used for years without any tangible results. Instead, you are ready to go the extra mile, experiment and test, while discovering your mistakes and improving on doing things better.

One of the stepping stones to achieving this feat is building positive self-talk. Since positive self-talk is a technique related to many other confidence barriers, we'll focus on other ways of building a growth mindset, then later, we shall discuss it in greater detail.

To build a growth mindset, first understand the true meaning of growth. Growth isn't a one-time thing; it is an ongoing process. Therefore, no matter how much you think you've grown, there will always be room for improvement.

Hence, you have to keep moving towards self-betterment. That said, this does not mean you should chase perfectionism. It only means you should embrace the idea of doing your best, looking for areas of growth and improvement, and then powering through by taking consistent action.

Next, rummage through your set of beliefs and pick any one of the most fixed beliefs. Write that down and explore it. What is it about that belief that does not sound or feel right to you? If you have written, "I can never become a millionaire," perhaps the thought of never becoming rich enough feels unsettling.

Eliminate the words with a negative connotation from this statement. In this case, omit 'never' from it, and rephrase it to read, "I can become a millionaire."

Tune into your feelings and see how you are really doing. How do you feel? Naturally, you will realize that you feel way better than before. Read the positive statement out aloud. Chant it 20-30 times, and don't just make it a one-off practice: practice it consistently.

Now, identify one area you can work on to achieve this goal. Saying powerful things works like magic, but the magic is everlasting only when you supply it with proof. After chanting the positive suggestion, complement it with real-time action.

So, if you desire to be a millionaire, find the one area that can help you move your money making needle. After identifying it, work on it every day.

With time, you will start seeing improvements and progress. You will no longer be stagnant but, will be moving towards growth.

Getting Beyond Unrealistic Goals

"90% of all disappointments come from unrealistic expectations."
— *Anonymous*

Dreaming big is a fundamental success doctrine. If you talk to every self-help guru, the common thread of advice you are likely to get is the essence of dreaming big and unlocking your imagination. While dreaming big, many of us make the common mistake of setting unrealistic goals and expectations.

Dreaming big and setting unrealistic goals are two different things that require proper segregation. Dreaming big is all about letting your imagination work for you without limitations. Dream of the impossible possibilities and beyond, so you can truly figure out what your heart desires. That's when you gain clarity on your vision and goals in life. Unless you dream big, and push the boundaries of what you think is possible, you will never discover what you are truly capable of.

To materialize those dreams, you have to set goals. Those goals can be bigger-than-life size, or smaller, bite-sized goals. This is important to ensure you can move towards your dreams in a step-by-step manner. During this process, some of us mistakenly set incredibly unrealistic goals and set even bigger expectations from them—and ourselves.

Perhaps your dream is to own a mansion in an exotic location, with hundreds of acres of land to your name. That's a lovely dream, yes, but setting the goal to achieve it all in under a month when you are not even earning $2000 a month is quite unrealistic. You need to leverage your imagination to scale up to the level of action required to hit your goal.

The problem with setting unrealistic goals is that they play with your sentiments. The adrenaline rush you experience because of extreme excitement puts you on cloud nine the first day, making you believe you can do everything. However, the rush wears off after a while. That's when reality starts to kick in, and when you see things pragmatically, you realize you weren't heading in the right direction and find the goal becoming too overwhelming.

The goal starts feeling difficult to achieve, and you start panicking. That's when the inevitable happens, and you decide to quit the pursuit. The instant you quit the pursuit, you might feel calmer, but also demotivated, and feeling like a failure.

You chastise yourself for failing to achieve what you wanted to achieve, a very unsettling feeling that can do a lot of damage to your internal wiring. When you experience low self-esteem because you failed to achieve your goals or dreams, this leads to the spiral of negative thinking that says: "You see, I told you it was pointless. You should have given it up when you had the chance."

You train your mind to *accept your failure as an inevitable outcome*, no matter how hard you try.

That's how unrealistic goals bury your confidence six feet under. You feel unsure and inadequate because you don't have a win to your credit. You spiral further into believing that failure is your destiny, and as you believe it, so it becomes. Remember, *you will always create your world from within no matter what the external circumstances are*.

The good thing is that this does not have to be your reality anymore. You don't need to continue feeling this continuity of repetitive failure. You deserve to feel happy, confident, strong, and successful. This guide is here to ensure that happens.

How to Set Realistic Goals

Setting unrealistic goals comes naturally to many of us. We let our dreams guide us and allow our thoughts to sway us in any possible direction.

To overcome the issue, here is a step-by-step process of what you need to do:

- Write down your ultimate dream very clearly. To figure that out, know what your life's vision is.

- What do you see yourself doing ultimately? Or where do you see yourself in 10 years? Write that down.

- Once you have that settled, think of how you plan to achieve that.

- Create a step-by-step process, more like an action guideline that leads to the end goal. For instance, if you see yourself as an environmentalist who runs a clean energy company, you need to set up your company, build a reputation, then ensure your business principles continue adding value to the environment. In this case, the first step would be to register and build your company. Once that is clear, you can determine the steps you need to take to make that happen.

- Once you have identified the first goal to work on, break it down into smaller parts. It is best to chop down the goal until it becomes small, manageable tasks that can be done in ten minutes or less. Goals only appear unrealistic when you view them as a whole, making them seem too big to achieve in this lifetime.

  However, they instantly seem less daunting when you make them doable by breaking them down into component pieces. Whatever your major goal is, keep breaking it down until the component pieces seem less overwhelming and manageable.

- Now, turn your goal into an objective. An objective is a mini goal with a pegged timeline. For example, when will you start working on the goal? When is it due? Write the start and end dates, thus ensuring you have a measurable and realistic deadline.

- Taking massive action is the only thing you have to do now. Get to it right now…you don't have time to waste!

Blame and Regret

When the subject of confidence comes up, 'blame' and 'regret' are two aspects not often discussed, primarily because many people do not think the two share any relationship.

How are blame and regret linked together?

Blame involves shifting responsibility to someone else for your problems. For example, if you did not get a job, you blame your partner for advising you to apply for a position that was challenging to get in the first place. If you incur a loss in your business, you may end up blaming your employees for not working hard enough, without considering that the job details and expectations you initially floated were not viable enough.

Whenever you declare someone else at fault for your wrongdoings, current issues, or unexpected experiences, you shift responsibility. Instead of accepting you are liable for a problem, you keep holding someone else accountable for it. Usually, when we do so, it is because taking responsibility feels difficult and somewhat traumatizing.

Blame is often all about not accepting a wrong move you made because that acceptance is in itself overpowering. Instead, you shift the blame to someone else. While this seems like an easy fix, it only debilitates your confidence.

"How," you might ask?

Because when you keep shifting responsibility, you keep moving away from your issues. Instead of addressing the real issues, you escape from them. The more you run away and evade, the bigger the fears inside you continue to grow. By doing this, you eventually get to a point where you cannot think about the issue because the fear has blown up into a mind filled with terror. What do you do then?

That's when most people only hold regrets in their hearts. You feel the time has passed, and since you feel like there's nothing you can do, you don't even try. With a remorseful heart, you only keep wishing you could go back in time, and as you know, time travel is not yet within our capacity (at least as far as we know to be true).

The regrets further weaken your confidence because, by that time, you are quite certain that success is not your destiny. You know things will only look bleak, and so, you decide not to try again. Your confidence keeps spiraling down, and so does your growth.

Let us now look at how you can move past blame and regret and become your confident self again.

How to Overcome Blame and Regret

It is a demanding process to move past blame and regret. Like most things in life, the process demands is time, patience, and consistency.

Overcoming blame and regret also demand that you lead from the forefront—not giving yourself a chance to avoid responsibility. Here are a set of steps you can implement right now to ensure you continue hacking away at this:

- Begin by describing the mess you are in at the moment. Whatever problems you may be facing right now, describe them in great depth in a journal.

- At the same time, think of what you feel remorseful about and why. Again, describe the scenario in detail. The more details you jot down, the better clarity you get on the overall scenario.

- Now ask yourself if you have been blaming someone else for them. Perhaps you hold your parents responsible for making you go to law school even though you are the one who made the final call. Write down why you hold the other person accountable for your issue.

- Continuing with the example above: if you blame your dad for making you study law while you wanted to pursue art, think of how he did not point a gun to your head. You are the one who agreed to do so in the end. Yes, he may be a controlling and manipulative man. But if you accept that you had a key role to play in making that decision, and it wasn't entirely your dad's fault, you would stop blaming him and start thinking in a manner that drives you towards self-betterment.

- Say the one thing you have been dreading for so long: "I accept my fault and take accountability for my decision."

- This confrontation can feel overpowering, but it is okay; let it all out. Sit with yourself for some time, and if you allow your emotions to calm down on their own, you will begin the process of emotional recovery.

- Once you complete this step, you will feel way lighter and calmer than before. What to do now?

- Think of how to cover up the mess in your life and improve on the situation. Perhaps if you are miserable as a lawyer, think of how to pursue art and make a living from it. Perhaps you can mix up the two by representing famous artists legally? The instant you shift your focus from being miserable to being responsible for your actions, ideas and opportunities start appearing.

Start working on this practice, and things will begin to turn around for you. Practice triggers momentum, and momentum funnels into energy that you can control.

The illusion that confidence is something you must wait for before taking action is a false dichotomy. You take action when scared, you take action when your mind is trying to hold you back, and in doing so, the "feeling" of confidence becomes your new drug of choice.

By doing something about the situation, you are taking on responsibility for everything. By taking total charge, you become the one in charge...of your own life.

Evaluating Perfectionism

"There is no space for peace when perfectionism is a priority." — **Christian Bosse**

If everything was perfect in this world, how would anyone bring about change—personal and social—or make a difference? How would we evaluate ourselves without any sense of accomplishment? In a Utopian world, what would be our higher purpose? Therefore, looking for "perfection" in a dystopian world equals nothing less than self-inflicted pain.

Perfectionism makes you think everything must be perfect and that you must comply with exceptionally high standards. As a result, you think your goals are unachievable and that, no matter what you do, you will never be good enough.

Perfectionists rely heavily on internal and external evaluation. However, they often fail to become self-satisfied and end up living unhappy lives. You may find yourself moving through such a stage in your life. The problem starts when you adopt constant perfectionism and view life from an "everything has to be perfect" perspective.

Having a perfectionist outlook is damaging. Imagine a situation where someone makes you feel that you can't achieve anything, or everything is out of your league. At first you will try to cope with what you have, but you cannot let that happen to you all the time. Eventually, you will distance yourself from that person and then shut them out.

Perfectionism doesn't allow you to celebrate your successes, small as they may be. Being a perfectionist is like having someone repeatedly tell you that you are imperfect, thereby reinforcing a level of perceived self-inadequacy.

Such a situation dismantles your self-esteem because of the many negative forces, like the sense of incapability and fear of disapproval that can pull you down. In turn, feeling this way produces high-density stress levels, and you feel incapable of focusing on your goals, ultimately feeling like a failure in life.

When do you think someone becomes conscious about being successful at everything he does?

When parental expectations are too high and rigid that they become oppressive. When your performance was overly praised, and you were taught to gauge your level of success based on your accomplishments. When you were constantly compared with better performers during your childhood. When perfection was a set standard from a young age, and guardians/parents punished you for not getting to the top academically.

How do you know if you struggle with perfectionism?

- You always think that you will never succeed at anything

- You can't stop procrastinating because every task is a big challenge that easily overwhelms you

- You can't stop feeling restless and often struggle to unwind

- You become very controlling when dealing with personal and professional relations

- You either take instructions and rules very well or immediately become disinterested

- You seek constant approval but still dissatisfied when you get it.

How to Overcome Perfectionism

The statement is simple: "allow yourself to settle for good enough." All you need to do is change how you look at the world.

- Pick any one of your pending tasks and write it down.

- Create columns in front of it and write headings like zero progress, task incomplete, partially meets expectations, meets expectations, and exceeds expectations.

- Monitor your progress daily

- When you view this table every day, it will motivate you to stop procrastinating and get down to work

- It will gradually influence you, helping you maintain your progress

- If you cannot get to the last level, tell yourself it's okay and pat yourself on the back for not leaving the task at zero progress.

- This way, you will manage to recognize your small daily efforts and praise yourself for them—and perhaps even reward yourself for the effort you've made so far.

- Don't restrict yourself to only one final appraisal and approval; instead, encourage yourself on the small steps you are taking towards the task every day

- Repeat this for every initiative you take from now on

Don't worry; this is not a permanent condition, and you can deal with it easily if you implement the simple plan above. All you have to do is be a little patient and consistently follow this plan. Make it a part of your daily routine.

People Pleasing

"When you engage in people-pleasing, you are out of integrity with yourself, your goals, your dreams, and your life's mission."

— **Eileen Anglin**

When you set your life objectives based on your will and aspirations, you can passionately pursue them. The main purpose is to get somewhere in life, achieve self-recognition, and be self-satisfied. The word "self" here suggests that what drives you to do this is the need to achieve individual contentment with "your" life.

Allowing external forces to hinder your progress is like letting others influence you. People-pleasing is different.

Here, you don't "permit" them to come in your way; you deliberately and knowingly "bring" them between yourself and your work. It's more like living *their* dreams when you seek *their* approval for everything.

The urge to please others is strongest in people who lack self-awareness and self-value and require others to evaluate them. The problem here is that you tend to "believe" what others have to say about you. If you were good at analyzing everyone's assessment, you wouldn't be out there pleasing everyone in the first place.

'Contemplation of feedback' is an art, and if you can't apply it to yourself, how can you expect to use it on others? You need to have a keen eye for this, and if you cannot observe and examine what's going on inside you, you will fail to clearly assess if that external judgment is valid or not.

Imagine having no control over what people say, and the only option you have to deal with it is to accept it? Such encounters shatter your confidence even further.

People-pleasing isn't just about letting others make statements about you. Being unable to say no to someone when they ask you for a favor is another prime example. It's how you try to make others happy with you, even if you have to ignore your comfort space and walk an extra mile for it.

The more you indulge in helping others, all while overlooking your own needs, the less self-confident you will start feel and behave. You will start perceiving your requirements as invaluable and have no one to blame but yourself for it. People-pleasers often feel helpless.

How to stop people-pleasing

To fix a problem, you need to deal with what's causing it. You end up pleasing others when you want to hear good views about yourself, which happens when you can't develop a self-opinion due to a lack of self-awareness. Since you want to hear nice comments about yourself, you are also willing to make people happy with you by never turning down their requests. And so, you become a slave to putting all those other needs and requests before your own needs.

You need to get to know yourself at a deeper level to avoid depending on others telling you who you are. You have to develop your capacity to validate your actions and goals in life "yourself." Above all, try to make yourself happy with "you."

Once you know where you stand, you will start being a good person only for "you," and that's the whole point of this discussion: to allow your self-regard and self-assumption to improve.

Following the guidelines below will allow you to kickstart a process that will help you overcome people-pleasing for good:

- Make a list of people close to you or who you think would invest in **you** to the same level.
- Don't be surprised if this list is very small.
- Be the same person to these people and start responding with "No" to the rest of the people around you.
- However, this doesn't mean you have to be disrespectful about it. All you have to do is say you won't be able to do it or try asking someone else. Try to acquire a friendly approach.
- Don't justify your "No" except with some people. You don't owe anyone any explanation in any sense; it's your right to say no when you don't want to do something for someone.
- To help yourself get started and be fully able to start saying "No," write down all the good qualities you have that you can think of at this exact moment. Try doing this for all domains like academically, personally, spiritually, financially, and socially.
- Try to bring improvement to this list. For this, you have to work on improving yourself and making yourself a better person overall.
- The problem with self-exploration is not that it's difficult; the problem is that you don't spend enough

time thinking about yourself. You feel "guilty" when you put yourself first.

- If you start doing so now, you'll eventually become addicted to making yourself the best version you can be.
- This will help you gain some insight into yourself, and you will start retrieving your confidence.

Designing this can take a day or two, but you will feel motivated once you have everything streamlined. You have catered to many peoples' needs for a long time; now it's your turn.

Low Self-esteem and Self-worth

"Self-esteem is the most fragile attribute in human nature. It can be damaged by very minor incidents, and its reconstruction is often difficult to engineer."

— Dr. James Dobson

Do you use the words "self-esteem" and "confidence" interchangeably? Are you aware of their differences?

Self-esteem is about being able to (respect) yourself the way you are, whereas confidence is about being capable of (believing) in yourself. To trust something, you have to regard it highly first. Therefore, a lack of self-respect makes you feel unassertive.

A sense of unworthiness stems from a disruption in early socialization. A family is a child's entire universe, which is why children grow to put all their trust in their families. Children view their parents' remarks as a standard by which to gauge themselves. If a child's family members make the child feel unimportant in any sense, it will leave its mark on the child.

A kid starts losing regard for his opinions when no one listens to him. He begins to lose respect for his capabilities when no one encourages his accomplishments. He tends to underestimate his potential when guardians, parents, or family members constantly compare him to better performers.

Developing confident personalities will be challenging if parents/guardians instill a sense of worthlessness in their minds during that phase. Growing up, the idea of being undeserving reinforces their perspective, and they eventually believe in it.

Low self-esteem and confidence don't necessarily revolve around everything in your life. It could be that you are unconfident about certain aspects of yourself, or not all. For instance, you can appreciate your intellect and constructive thinking, but be self-conscious about your appearance and looks.

The rule is simple: **When you cannot develop respect for something, you can't believe in it.**

How to Build Self-esteem and Self-worth

There are many ways to elevate your self-esteem and sense of self-worth, but here, we will stick to just one strategy for now:

- The first step is to accept that everything has elements of perfection and faults at the same time.

- Learn to accept who you are as a person. To do this, you need to describe yourself in a few words.

- Write down who you think you are: flaws, strengths, and character traits. Yes, there must be strengths because you most certainly have them.

- After doing this, simply say: "I accept myself fully and wholeheartedly."

- Chant this mantra about ten times, or until you start feeling good about yourself.

- At the same time, write down the personal features that make you very proud of yourself, and be thankful for them.

- Gratitude is positive energy that makes you aware of how abundantly blessed you are—even when it doesn't feel so.

- Nurturing gratitude will give you the motivation to deal with your self-perceived deficiencies effectively.

Work on this strategy regularly, and at the same time, reflect more on your weaknesses on how to improve them. The next chapter shares a confidence-boosting activity that further builds on this practice.

Failed Expectations

"Frustration is the result of failed expectations."

— Stuart Kidder

We often fall below our own—and other peoples' expectations—of us. Therefore, the disappointment you feel afterward is either internal or external. These are the only two sources where you receive this wave of desolation that affects your self-esteem and internal belief system.

Internal dissatisfaction occurs when you set very high expectations for yourself and, fail to achieve what you have formed in your mind regarding those expectations.

To be fully satisfied with yourself, you need to meet your own expectations. Happiness results from exceedingly met expectations that results from progress. However, if the result is something below your average presumption, you become disappointed with yourself, and dissatisfied with the results.

Whether you get a good (desirable) result or a bad (undesirable) result is not the issue, and it should not sway your happiness meter. What truly matters is that you tried something, you moved forward by taking intentional action, and whether it turned out the way you were expecting is irrelevant. The only measure of success is moving forward. The only measure for failure is not doing anything.

You can form two types of internal expectations that have a high chance of resulting in disappointment. First, you can set unrealistic goals beyond your potential, or not in the right field. In both cases, even if you try your level best and spare no effort to achieve them, the turnout is usually dissatisfactory. The reason is not your incapacity to work, but rather, your inability to set an achievable goal.

Once your endeavors seem like a waste of time to you, you start struggling to pursue your objective with greater enthusiasm. Your experience starts to pull you back, making you feel unconfident, that it will not be worth the effort.

The only driving force that motivates us to proceed towards our targets is our love for the target. The question then becomes, "how can you love your work when you are unable to see any achievement or success in the future?" One poor experience that failed your expectations, and you gradually start to lose confidence in yourself. You see failure everywhere. You want to stop trying because you might experience that feeling of failing again…and again.

Second, we have an external influence. At times, you cannot meet society's expectations, which leaves you feeling terrible inside. People think highly of someone who has excelled in a specific field or someone good at something for a long time.

Failing to live up to these expectations involves a factor of external disapproval, which happens when a person thinks that he has lost social recognition. This discrepancy affects the person's self-worth, and the person then considers the whole image rebuilding process too tiresome and demanding.

If one negative experience decreases your confidence, imagine how having several of them would affect you? People let such instances get to them and fall into this trap of helplessness.

How to Deal with Unmet Expectations

The solution is rewarding, but it takes committed effort. If you want to get past such experiences, here is what you have to do:

- Think of and write down the number of times you have successfully satisfied what you and people around you were anticipating

- Then jot down the number of times you failed to meet expectations, both internally and externally, then compare the two lists.

- Encourage yourself for the fortunate attempts and scrutinize where you went wrong for the unsuccessful ones.

- Remind yourself that failure is only failure if you choose not to learn from it and better yourself.

Some encounters will carry more emotional weight, making them a struggle to let go of or overcome. When you come across these struggles, remind yourself that you're the only one who can deal with them.

Remind yourself that you're the only one who knows your fears better than anyone and, therefore, the only one who can do something worthwhile about them; then, once you accept this, motivate yourself to take small steps towards becoming a better you.

CHILDHOOD WOUNDS AND SELF-IMPOSED LIMITATIONS

Do you have a specific habit you can't justify? Has someone ever accused you of behaving a certain way? Do you think everyone thinks the same about a particular mannerism you have? If you have such questions in mind, it could be due to some negative interference with your upbringing.

While there are various types of childhood traumas, the concept behind their emergence is the same. When, as a child, you start walking and socializing with society, you don't know how the world functions, or what it expects of you. You don't know which goals and intentions to have and, most importantly, what to expect from yourself and others, nor do you know much about most of what happens around you.

During this phase, you absorb information from external sources. These external sources can be your immediate family, media, teachers, and friends. Conscience building starts at the age of three, and the first five years of your life as a child are critical. Besides absorbing information from your environment, you also absorb your parents' mindsets and the related thoughts and beliefs.

It's very damaging for a child when parents act out aggressively with anger, shouting, frustration or verbal abuse. During (and after) this phase, failing to live in a nurturing environment is likely to have a negative impact on your self-esteem in the long term.

Neglect, ignorance, feeling deprived of love and care, being on the receiving end of constant yelling and criticism, gradually chips away at and weakens your self-belief, denying it the chance to grow. If you experience any form of bullying or endure childhood abuse, those experiences are likely to leave a lasting impact on your internal confidence.

You are likely to indulge in setting self-inflicting restrictions on yourself because you grew up that way. The childhood wounds you had may have healed with time, but if you lack faith in yourself, the pain is still there, beneath the surface of your emotions, still deeply tied to that past trauma. To start feeling comfortable with who you are, and developing a healthy self-love for yourself, you must work on resolving that trauma.

How to Overcome Mental Barriers

As mentioned earlier, you don't start feeling unconfident on your own; someone makes you feel that way. It could be a friend, family, a coach or teacher, or tuning into negative messages from the media. These negative influencers leave a lasting impact on you that can stick with you for the rest of your life if you don't course correct.

But you can reprogram your learning. Just because you were raised a certain way, to believe certain things about yourself, it doesn't mean you have to stick with it.

Consider integrating the following points to begin repairing your mental hurdles:

- You cannot change your past to better yourself. However, that shouldn't be an excuse to dwell on it.

- Accept it and love yourself as you are. But, don't settle for staying where you are. Point your compass true North and get moving.

- Let go of old resentments and forgive those who did that to you.

- Put an end to the habit of negative self-talk. Replace this habit with positive words of empowerment to make your brain register the change you have decided to make. This will start the process that will help you move forward.

Regaining Confidence in Toxic Relationships

"The idea is quite simple, stay a light year away from people who make you feel less about yourself." — Mohith Agadi

Imagine being around people who love you. Imagine a wholesome love that makes you better than your yesterday's self. Or being in an environment where giving more than receiving feels natural instead of the compulsion or fear of consequence.

Imagine being in relationships where your growth as a human being is a shared interest instead of wishful thinking, where everyone celebrates your joys and accomplishments, and you thrive as a person and as part of a community.

Now, imagine the absence of that love. Imagine yourself in a situation where you live in a selfish relationship that takes from you more than you receive in return, feels void, and breaks you down as a person. Imagine a situation where you feel better off without it, but thinking about walking away leaves you with feelings of guilt.

The first victim of a toxic relationship is your confidence and self-esteem. Such a relationship makes you feel like a lesser person, and your opinions are invalidated. In such a relationship, every bad thing that happens becomes your fault, even when the core responsibility lies with the other person. Your relationship partner guilt-trips you into thinking and doing things that aren't essentially "you" but what the toxic person wants from you.

Some toxic relationships are glaringly obvious and full of visible emotional, verbal, and sometimes physical abuse. In contrast, other toxic relationships are so subtle that the manipulation takes ages to register in your mind. In these relationships, the manipulation becomes so normalized in your life that it doesn't even feel like a bad thing; it feels like a routine treatment.

Identifying toxic people and relationships in your life can be difficult. It takes courage to pinpoint people who turn you into a version of yourself that you dislike. Emotional abuse has a way of concealing itself in the guise of a normal relationship. The familiarity of it feels comfortable because it is what you know, even if it makes you unhappy. Your emotional dependence on the other person leaves you ill-equipped to see the abuse for what it is.

An important thing to note is that, not all toxic people are bullies or cruel people. They are just people who are forcefully implementing their vision of how the world around them should be, and you happen to be under their toxic influence because of your proximity to them. These people are the bane of everyone's happiness, and not just yours.

How to Let Go of Toxic Relationships

You can find a lot of advice on cutting off toxic people from your life. You hear it every day. In all honesty, doing that is easier said than done—we have already discussed how identifying toxic relationships isn't always a straightforward process because of your dependence on them.

Now let's take a look at how to do that:

- Think of all the times a particular person made you feel so terrible about yourself that it made you completely lose your confidence.

- Visualize how different the situation would have turned out if they hadn't done that.

- Let that guide you into setting **healthy boundaries** for yourself.

- Identify where you draw the line for the influence you can allow other people to have on you from now on.

- Communicate your boundaries. Don't allow people to overstep the lines you have put in place.

- Remind them that things have changed, and they need to respect your new assertions.

- If they continue with their old behavior, cut them off. Block, delete, and ignore them.

- You don't always have to justify your decision to distance yourself from people because most know what they have done—they just don't want to admit it out loud. This burden is not on you.

You will notice that distancing yourself from negativity changes you as a person. For example, you are likely to feel more self-assuredness and assertiveness as you get control over your thoughts, opinions, and actions.

It feels liberating to cleanse your life of negative and toxic people. No matter how close you are to a person, don't let anyone hold you back from living your true self.

Confidence Myths Holding You Back

"You need to be born confident."

"You can't fake confidence."

"You have to be successful to be confident."

"You have to be an extrovert to be confident."

"Confident people have no insecurities."

Have you come across such statements, or do you actively believe in them? Some of you must have questions and contradictions regarding these in mind. Some of you might have accepted yourselves as you are according to such myths. Some of you might be reading about them for the first time here. But all I have to say about this is simple: please do not have faith in such sentiments.

These are nothing but words of fallacy and misconception, most likely made by people who took pride in their confidence and who wanted to have supremacy over others. By floating such misinterpretation among people, they try to form an impression that no one can be like them. The way it makes you feel is exactly the purpose behind their formation, mostly done for self-consolation.

Do not fall into this trap. Always try to understand and question why something is said or done a particular way. Do not let such censure get to you. Such beliefs serve as major inhibitors to your untapped potential.

You will never get past a certain level of confidence if you stick to limiting concepts and beliefs. Besides, the more you believe in these superstitions, the more your confidence shrinks, as these ideas form your belief system around what you think is possible and impossible.

My goal—and your focus—for this challenge is to question everything. Train your brain to recognize the false fallacies of self-defeating ideas that tear down your confidence. The greatest dreams are always built on believing in what was once seemingly an impossible climb.

How to Unlearn So You Can Learn

The answer to this question is simple:

- Accept that confidence is something you "can" build.

- Once you start believing in this, you will subconsciously begin to ignore such absurd claims.

- Pay no heed to it and start passionately moving towards building faith in yourself.

- All it needs is commitment and regular practice.

- Ignore any such incoherent assertions and work on overcoming the rest of the roadblocks to confidence.

At this point, how you keep yourself from becoming confident should be abundantly clear. When it comes to confidence, there is not just one, but several types of confidence you should be aware of.

Let's push forward and, in the next section, you will learn the different types of self-confidence.

Part 2: The Types of Confidence

"Life is not easy for any of us. But what of that? We must have perseverance and above all confidence in ourselves. We must believe that we are gifted for something and that this thing must be attained."

— Marie Curie

"At the end of the day, the king and the pawn go in the same box."

— **Italian Proverb**

The Social Status of Confidence

This profound Italian proverb hits home. It shows how we each stand on the pedestal of equality and are all born foundationally equal.

Nevertheless, none of us can fight the fact that a king and pawn have different statuses. If you analyze the two, you will realize that the differences in status come from the value the two impart around. As you dig deeper into the equation, you'll realize that the value the king offers to those around him depends on his confidence—mostly in his capacity as a king.

A king's confidence is on an entirely different level than that of a pawn. A king knows how capable and competent he is. He is 100% sure of his competence, and how much he benefits those around him. This is why he can maintain his position as a king.

On the other hand, a pawn does not share the same status as the king. He may be way more capable than the king, but if he cannot position himself as someone worth the power and the competence, he can't contest for that position.

If you want to win in life and go far in all your pursuits, you need to be as confident as a king. This also goes to show that confidence is a prerequisite to living a quality life driven by intentional choices.

Confidence is packaged in different forms. Let's take a look at the types of confidence available to you in this chapter...

Social Confidence

Social confidence refers to being confident in social settings. If you are socially confident, you do not shy away from discussions in social settings. Rather, you take the lead and are emotionally, physically, and mentally present and active in every conversation. You might project the image of someone whom is the authority on a topic, adding your valuable insight to the discussion as others listen and learn from you.

As confident and enthusiastic as you appear in social settings, you tend to be the complete opposite when at home. You tend to be quiet at home and mostly live in your bunker.

Similarly, you may not be too active in your relationships, be it those with your friends, partner, family members, and coworkers. You may not talk or mingle with people often but prefer solitary time to think and process your ideas and thoughts. Your social confidence extends from the ability to go deep in your thinking, analyzing your thoughts and programming your mind for the next social encounter.

Then, after spending enough time reenergizing, the instant you are in a social setting, you are a completely different person: poised, intuitive, talkative, energetic and engaging.

Self-Centered Confidence

Often called 'cockiness,' self-centered confidence occurs when confidence is blown out of proportion. It usually happens when you feel so overconfident in your confidence that you disregard all those around you. In the case of self-centered confidence, you tend to overpraise yourself to the point that it becomes an extreme and uncomfortable situation for everyone around you.

This egotistical or selfish approach, self-centered confidence makes you go after your vested interests. No matter what you do or wherever you are, you can only think and talk about yourself. Every time you start talking about something, you either begin with your accomplishments or, find a way to steer the conversation towards yourself.

In the end, it is always about you. Guess what, nobody likes that. People pick up on it and try to avoid you at social gatherings or passing on the street.

Being egotistic comes from self-obsession. It's all about being obsessed with yourself, and mostly, the idea of yourself. You see yourself as someone superior to everybody else and cannot stand it when someone seems to grow bigger or better than you.

Self-absorption can sometimes lead to narcissism, which is a state characterized by having an inflated sense of self-esteem. In the case of narcissism, you consider other people inferior and cannot nurture a healthy compassion or empathy for others. Besides that, most narcissists are very talented but don't have many accomplishments to their credit.

PERFECTION-SEEKING CONFIDENCE

Perfection-seeking confidence makes you pursue perfectionism in everything you undertake. This kind of confidence has both pros and cons, but taken to the extreme, it does more harm than good.

This confidence is the belief that you need to be perfect in everything you do, and that you must perform well in every area to become (and remain) self-assured and successful.

You want to be unshakable, and you believe the only way to accomplish that is to master everything. This is the result of what happens to people who are trapped in the 'perfection cycle."

This type of self-confidence is easy to find on social media nowadays. It manifests as the hype revolving around doing and being more, being independent, hustling hard, and always trying to achieve more.

Now, there is nothing wrong with being a hustler, trying to achieve your dreams, or being an independent mover and a shaker. However, the perception and attitude that you must do everything to the letter in order to be confident and happy in order to reach your goals can lead to an unhealthy balance.

What if you get stuck in a terrible job you hate in this process? What if trying to perfect everything means you keep looking for hope in a dead relationship that only brings you misery? What if you spend year chasing money, only to get it and still experience low self-esteem and confidence?

These are the other sides of the story you must consider. Striving to be confident and happy is important, but never at the cost of your mental well-being.

To be confident in its truest sense means you are confident at all times- in times when you are doing well, and in times when the going gets tough, and you have to dig in with grit to beat your way through with mental toughness leading the way.

Superior Confidence / Inferior Confidence

Since the two are interrelated, it is best to discuss them together.

Superior confidence—illusory confidence—is a state where you see yourself as superior to everyone else and tend to look down upon others. On the other hand, inferior confidence—illusory inferiority—is where you feel you are not good enough, lack potential and talent, and don't measure up to others.

Both states are detrimental to your well-being. "How," you may ask?

Well, superior confidence makes you self-absorbed. Even if you are capable, when you become self-seeking, you only work for your vested interests. In this process, you are likely to ignore others, and disregard their efforts as well.

As for illusory inferiority, you lack confidence and feel you can never be good enough. In this case, you downplay your biggest strengths and never give yourself the due credit you deserve as well.

CONTROLLING CONFIDENCE

This type of confidence relates to illusory confidence—it is one of its most common symptoms—but here, you become controlling to the extent that you want everything to be perfect. Driven by the desire to feel and become superior, you start controlling things. In this process, you strive to ensure that everything goes just as planned, all so that you don't lose your state of superiority.

You may feel good about yourself for some time during this process, but things tend to become more difficult for you in the long run. Moreover, your controlling demeanor makes you a difficult person for others to be around. You most likely criticize everything and everyone around you, which people find off-putting.

Self-Sabotage Confidence

Also called the 'backfire effect,' this confidence type involves failing at things that have a long-term negative impact, such as gambling, or binging on junk food just after losing ten pounds. Even then, you carry on with that behavior confidently, often driven by the belief that you will eventually achieve success in that negative and unhealthy practice.

In most cases, this cycle continues with a very long string of dissimilar failures in several key areas of life: relationships, career, personal endeavors, and can negatively impact your mental and physical environment.

Self-sabotage confidence also refers to engaging in behaviors that weaken your confidence. For instance, you may have a habit of repeatedly questioning your potential. You may feel that doing so helps you improve, but in reality, it weakens your self-confidence because you constantly doubt yourself.

Simulation Confidence

This is a type of confidence you pretend to have but don't have in reality. You try to trick your mind into believing that you are confident and strong, whereas, in reality, you are only struggling to achieve that state. Its most common name is the "fake it till to make it" strategy.

Simulation confidence is a helpful way to build confidence. Usually, when you try to fake it till you make it, you end up making it. This is why experts often advise us to imagine being confident or to keep smiling till we start feeling happy. For example, during flight simulations, instructors often ask pilots to fake a scenario in the sky to feel confident.

However, this strategy works well only when you truly believe you are confident, happy, successful or whatever you are trying to fake.

SITUATIONAL CONFIDENCE

Not everybody is competent in everything, and that's okay too. That said, there may be something you feel confident in or doing. Perhaps you feel confident in your marketing skills. Maybe you are a confident swimmer or a confident public speaker. While you may be confident in these areas, it is also possible to feel unconfident in other areas of your life, such as your relationships, financial management, or handling difficult coworkers.

This state where you are confident in one area but lacking poise in another is what we refer to as 'situational confidence.'

Different types of situational confidence include the following:

- **Cognitive confidence**: This is when you feel confident about your intellect and cognitive abilities.

- **Health confidence**: This is a state of confidence where you feel good about your physical health and capabilities.

- **Educational confidence**: This is when you feel confident about your academics and educational capabilities.

The gist of situational confidence is that your confidence varies from situation to situation. Situational confidence is not a negative state nor a sign of weakness. However, it is important to shape your confidence in different aspects of your life to ensure you feel totally confident, and not just in random situations or near familiar people.

The test of your confidence is not in comfortable situations, but rather, confronting the challenge of facing discomfort. It is through successfully handling difficult and uncomfortable situations with poise and integrity that your confidence is taken to the next level.

Foundational Self-Confidence

Foundational self-confidence is the ultimate kind of confidence we are trying to seek and build. Having foundational confidence is crucial because it helps you start feeling good in your judgment, personality, knowledge, and abilities. This confidence is also the base for your overall confidence, making it more or less like a confidence conduit.

Foundational confidence is the kind of confidence you need to work on developing. When you have—and continue— nurturing foundational confidence, it slowly grows into a huge tree of confidence, one that spreads its shade around, comforts others, and provides a safe space for you to be yourself. This shade of confidence expands when you continuously push outside of your comfort zone and continue to *Do the Hard Things First*.

Foundational self-confidence is something you must nurture and tend to in the right manner. Things will go haywire when you don't stoke your foundational confidence, and you may develop a superiority complex, narcissism, and other life-impacting issues.

Before moving on to an activity that'll help enhance your self-confidence, let me quickly throw some light on what being self-confident can truly do for you.

How Life Changes for the Better When You are Confident

Life changes for the better when you are amazingly confident, and let me tell you exactly how:

(1) You Become Happier

Most people think that the direct positive outcome of being confident is gaining respect, being appreciated, and attaining success. Seldom do they associate happiness with it, and instead, most people associate happiness with well-being, life satisfaction, relationships, fulfilling careers, and having good friends. The reality is that confidence and happiness have a robust connection.

A study conducted in 2014 examined the self-esteem and happiness levels of 200 students. Researchers observed that, even the slightest increase in one's sense of self-esteem boosted their overall sense of happiness. Another small-scale research study from Ireland reveals the same.

The research paper "Does Self-Esteem Cause Better Performance, Interpersonal Success, Happiness or Healthier Lifestyle?' by Prof. Roy Baumeister is one of the most cited papers on the subject. It showed that self-esteem is one of the most substantial factors in predicting life satisfaction in over 31,000 college students.

Confidence leads to happiness in the sense that when you think well of yourself and know you are capable of doing what you want and following through with your heart's deepest and most genuine desires, you can feel motivated to take action. As a result, you find yourself doing things that bring you pure joy.

A Deep Feeling of Empowerment

Empowerment comes from being able to make choices for yourself and being able to make those calls. Once you feel empowered, you can easily decide things for yourself and own your decisions, something that cannot happen without self-confidence.

When you feel sure in yourself, know what you want, and like yourself enough to do what you please, it becomes easier to make personal, career, and life decisions that move you closer to your ultimate dreams.

As you start to call the shots in your life, you feel empowered in yourself, and your life becomes more about what you want instead of how others want you to be. That's how confidence leads to an empowered and high-quality life.

Sustainable Career Progression

Career progression depends greatly on making the right move at the right time, or, making a move right after making the first one. It also depends on seeking different opportunities and then actively pursuing them. You cannot expect to climb the success ladder in your career if you keep sitting in one corner without doing anything worthwhile to achieve career progression.

The important point to highlight here is that you only feel strong enough to move around, raise your voice, ask for things, mingle with people, and exercise your rights when you feel confident. Without feeling self-assured and having a high but healthy opinion of yourself, you won't even take these steps; and when you don't engage in these practices, you won't achieve the desired career progress.

If you analyze the lives of those faring well in their lives and achieving wealth from their professional pursuits, you will notice that what sets them apart isn't their "privileged status"' most of them have none. What truly sets them apart is believing in themselves and having complete faith in their capabilities.

They may not always be the best at everything, but they are sure they can learn and grow—growth-minded. This drive encourages these people to engage in constant self-improvement that strengthens their confidence. As a result, they successfully find and leverage great opportunities.

THE OPPORTUNITY TO CREATE THRIVING RELATIONSHIPS

The foundation of healthy, happy, and long-lasting relationships is a combination of respect, love, understanding, trust, and equality. To this equation, I'd like to add one more element: self-belief.

Relationships need love, passion, understanding, trust, and a lot more to work and thrive. Whether it is your relationship with your sibling, parent, spouse, or friend, if you don't understand each other, spend quality time with each other, and bring something exciting to the table, the relationship will lose its luster.

To be able to do all that, you need to first believe in yourself. If you are going through confidence issues that make you doubt yourself, you will feel stuck and stagnant in life.

For example, your partner may want to spend some time with you, but you will be busy worrying about self-created tensions. Your kids may want you to take them out, but you'll be busy worrying about the lack of growth in your career. This gives your lack of confidence a chance to consume your peace of mind and relationships. After all, if you are battling personal issues, you won't have any strength left to cater to those around you.

On the other hand, when you are confident, you can focus well on your relationships, understand the needs of every relationship, address each need—and relationship problem—calmly, work on strengthening the bond, and pour out more love and respect. Always remember that you can never pour from an empty cup.

Leverage Your Strengths and Overcome Your Weaknesses

The key to doing consistently well in life is consistent self-improvement. If you think you are perfect, you are likely to never improve on your shortcomings. When you deliberately overlook your shortcomings, you can develop a grandiose sense of self that, as mentioned earlier, can negatively affect your confidence levels.

You may not realize it right away, but sooner or later, you will experience some problems sooner or later, such as making uninformed decisions or acting too hastily—often to preserve your idealized sense of self.

On the other hand, if you don't take stock of your strengths, you will never give yourself the due credit and appreciation you deserve. You are likely to wallow in misery, always cribbing about how growth and success never become your destiny, not realizing that you are not genuinely working towards the two.

You need to conduct a self-assessment regularly to know what you are good at and where you lack. Doing this allows you to polish your strengths, and at the same time, overcome your weaknesses or turn them into strengths.

As a result, you become a greater version of yourself and further raise your self-esteem.

Achieve Your Goals and Aspirations

Naturally, as you become a greater and more qualified, capable version of yourself, you focus in on your goals and targets with better accuracy. Previously, you may not have been able to handle certain tasks, but you will now have the capacity to do so.

For example, after conducting a detailed assessment of your shortcomings, you may realize that you have always wanted to own and run a company but couldn't because you felt you lacked leadership skills. Once you realize this and start working on those issues, you will feel better equipped to run your firm like a boss.

When you constantly improve yourself and fix your shortcomings, you become more focused and energetic. You know what you want in life and are certain about how you can achieve it.

When your focus becomes crystal clear, you become more productive as well. You start to manage time efficiently, which increases your productivity, output, and progress in all your endeavors, particularly the professional ones.

By now, you must be well aware of what confidence can do for you and how it can breathe comfort, value, meaning, and tranquility in your life.

Let's get to work on an activity that helps you become truly confident.

Confidence Building Exercise

For this activity, first, make an intention of thinking actively and jotting down your ideas in a journal or notebook. There are blank pages provided at the back of this book for you to use. Whatever way you choose, make sure to write down your notes right away to ensure that you do not forget or miss out on anything.

Identify 3 areas of confidence you excel in. First, write down any three areas of confidence you are exceptionally good at—to simplify, analyze any three aspects of your life that you feel confident in, and describe them.

For instance, if you are a confident speaker, that could be one area. If you are confident in your relationship with your child, that could be the second area. If you feel you are a confident cook who makes excellent dishes, that could be the third area.

Now, use these examples with yourself and write that here:

1.

2.

3.

Rank Yourself from 1 to 10

Now, rank yourself in those three areas you identified on a level of 1 to 10, with 1 being the lowest and 10 being the highest.

Write down each area and assess yourself accordingly.

Describe *how you feel* about yourself

How do you feel about yourself right now? Do you feel good about yourself and happy to see that you are at least faring well in some areas of your life?

If earlier you were feeling low or sad about yourself and did not quite approve of yourself, you are likely to feel positive right now and capable enough to do what you want in life.

Now move in the opposite direction, and think of the areas you need to be more confident in. Think of any aspects of your life you don't feel too confident in.

Perhaps you are not too confident in your academics. You feel you may not pass your Physics exam because you are not too good at the subject.

Maybe you are not confident in front of the camera. Since your job often requires you to appear in videos, this is one area you would like to improve.

Perhaps you are not too confident in your relationship with your spouse. You feel it has strained over the past few years and that it is losing the magic it once had.

Think of your life and its various aspects, and then, write down which areas you need to work on to brush up your confidence.

Now, think of why these areas matter to you and how motivated you are to improve your confidence in them.

If your relationship with your partner is important to you, but it was once full of a love you don't want to lose, describe those feelings. Reflect on whether you genuinely want to save and continue with that relationship. The same applies to the other areas you identified above.

Next, think about what you feel you can do to bring about the desired improvement in those areas. Focus on achieving just 1% growth every month and move forward with your plan of action.

For instance, if you are not a confident speaker yet, perhaps you can start speaking in front of a small group of people for now. Once you do that, you will notice a natural demeanor improvement. Once you can speak in front of 2 to 5 people, you can move to slightly bigger gatherings, and as you experience gradual improvements, start speaking in front of a camera.

Go ahead and share your self-improvement strategies and plans below. Doing this will solidify your plan and commitment. Most of us make big plans every day but fall short of achieving them, not because the plans are not good, or we lack any potential to fulfill them, but because we often forget them.

For example, you may forget how you decided to work on a goal, your intention to send an email to a client, or your commitment to speak to a group of twenty people.

When you forget to take action on things you deem important, it instantly affects your confidence negatively because you are not taking the required action to move towards self-betterment and growth.

Next, take things a step further and start taking the desired action because, without taking intentional action, you won't get the results you desire.

How do you plan to take action? Write a brief action plan of that in your notebook.

For instance, let's say you plan to speak to a group of people. How will you select that group? What will you talk about? When will the speaking engagement take place? Can it happen anywhere or at any time? Write down all these pointers and reflect on every possible aspect of that activity to enhance your clarity.

Trust me; things become easy when you have clarity on what you wish to do and your proposal to tackle it. We only feel confused when we don't know what we want. The instant we get some clarity, it becomes simple to move towards our desired goal.

Work on this final step of the exercise and write down every possible step related to what you wish to do regarding becoming more confident in the identified areas, then take one step at a time.

For example, if you want to make your videos, this is the area where you wish to become more confident. Write that down, and then write down the steps you identified above.

For each of those steps, describe what, why, where, how, and when you will do it:

Step 1:

Step 2:

Step 3:

Now that we have that part figured out, it is time to take action. This entire book focuses on helping you empower your confidence and take the necessary action too. Since we have been engaging in an exercise here, it is important to give you an action tip you can use to take action; otherwise, you won't feel charged enough to take the desired steps.

So, here's what you have to do:

- Take any of the action tips mentioned above. For example, if you have decided to talk to five people every day, do that now.

- Now hammer that into an even smaller bit. For example, right now, you have to identify the five people you want to talk to.

- Write down the names of people you feel comfortable talking to. If you are falling short of one individual, think of what you need to do to find that or how you can find one more person for your group.

- Now take that very action. If you have decided to look for someone on social media, send away that post now. If you need to send an email, do it right away. Once you take the smallest of action right away, you feel peace flowing in your system, and that's how you kick start the journey to empowering your self-confidence.

With this part of the training on confidence covered, let us move to the next part of the book that teaches you how to **reinvent your neuroplasticity and confidence**.

Part 3: Reinventing Your Confidence, Brain and Neuroplasticity

"Confidence is not 'they will like me.' Confidence is, 'I'll be fine if they don't.''

— **Anonymous**

"It took me fifteen years to discover that I had no talent for writing, but I couldn't give it up because by that time I was too famous."

— **Robert Benchley**

Believing In Confidence

Confidence is about believing you will be totally fine, even if the world around you does not approve of you. That's because when you become confident, your happiness does not depend on what others think and feel about you. It depends entirely on how you feel about yourself. It's the relationship you have with yourself that determines the stability of your confidence.

Confidence is how you feel about yourself when you're alone with yourself.

Gaining that belief is not easy because rewiring the brain to think optimistically, especially when you have constantly been disparaging yourself most of your life, is a lengthy process.

If you are willing to do the work, you can work on changing that for the better. Even if you are unwilling to realize and accept this now, you have the power to control your thoughts and change them for the better. You can focus on behaviors that help you reinforce your faith, create new beliefs to reinforce your goals, and concentrate on the good things in life. You can develop better habits and make incremental progress every day for the rest of your life.

As you read this section of the book, you will learn to rewire your brain for confidence way beyond your wildest dreams. You will learn to generate the energy necessary for developing a life of fulfillment—the true path to a confident and happier lifestyle.

To get started, let's take a deep dive into the power of neuroplasticity and your brain's amazing capacity to rewire itself to think a certain way.

Understanding Neuroplasticity

Neuroplasticity is a basic concept that underpins various learning experiences. It is your brain's fundamental ability to modify itself and reorganize itself based on your previous, ongoing, and future life experiences.

For the longest time, scientists truly believed that humans had a "fixed brain." In other words, they believed the brain was not plasticity, that it could not change or mold itself differently.

However, the latest research, fMRI scans, and many studies have proven that the human brain remains enigmatic. It is indeed malleable, which means it is flexible and adaptable. This discovery gave birth to the term neuroplasticity: neuro encompasses the brain and nervous system, and plastic comes from the word plasto, a word of Greek origin that means changeable.

The Human Brain is Adaptable

Neuroscience is now uncovering scores of new realizations about the mysterious human brain every other month. Modern-day neuroscientists have now revealed that the human brain has billions of brain cells, called neurons, that can connect with thousands of other brain cells simultaneously.

Every neuron is potentially capable of forming thousands of connections and synapses with other neurons. These connections offer tons of other opportunities for communication and connection within the brain. This also means that the more connections you make, the more room for growth and change there is. Hence, there is extensive room for development and learning in the human brain.

Every time you experience or learn something new, the neurons in your brain form one or more new neuronal connections. Since the connections are constantly changing, the brain experiences neuroplasticity, which makes it capable of changing, molding, and adapting to the new set of experiences you go through.

This is how the brain harnesses the power of neuroplasticity. In the simplest terms possible, if only one of the billions of neurons in your brain releases a neurotransmitter that can connect with and activate a receptor, it forms a connection.

When you use one connection regularly, it reinforces that particular neuronal pathway, making the neuronal connection stronger and effortless too, which makes engaging in that action easier for you. This is how we form habits. When you repeatedly engage in a certain practice, its particular neuronal pathways become stronger, and you start to engage in it on autopilot mode.

In contrast, when you don't use a certain neuro pathway regularly, the connection weakens with time, slowly fading away. As the connection weakens, so does the practice associated with it.

This implies several things:

- ☐ Your brain is forever changing. The different experiences you have in life constantly shape it.

- ☐ Whenever you engage in a certain practice, it forms a neuronal connection.

- ☐ If the experience is new and novel, it forms a new connection. If you have previously engaged in the activity, it strengthens the same connection.

- ☐ Neural connections strengthen or weaken depending on how frequently you engage in that activity.

What connection does this have with rewiring your brain to think positively and shaping your confidence?

Let's dive deeper into what this means.

The Connection between Neuroplasticity and Confidence

As we have discussed, neuroplasticity is your brain's capacity to change. If you have previously been feeling unconfident or have gone through circumstances in life that have strained your sense of self-esteem, it is not the end of the world.

Yes, you have engaged in activities that have tarnished your confidence, and now those practices come naturally to you because you have built those habits. That said, you can still change the neuronal connections and form new ones that breathe confidence, ease, value, and meaning into your life.

Losing confidence does not mean this is your fate. Your life—and its course—are in your hands. You can easily change it in any way you like, provided you genuinely and truly want to improve for the better.

Always remember that 'neurons that fire together, wire together.' In essence, when you fire up a neuronal connection in your brain, you create a new wiring system, and this wiring will solidify with time if you keep taking that action. Thus, to build self-confidence, you need to engage in practices that shape your brain's neuroplasticity for the better and make it more adaptable to a positive environment.

Understand and accept a simple fact: **your brain has the power to reshape itself.** You can make your brain think and behave any way you want it to because it is not at all rigid. That is how you can bring about real, transformative change into your life.

Fortunately, there is more than one way to make that happen. You can implement different strategies and exercises to actualize this result, but it is possible. Once you commit to taking consistent action, with time, you'll notice that, by transforming your mental environment, your confidence will rise to a whole new level.

So, are you ready to do this?

Are you ready to start a new journey in your life where you will actively shape your confidence?

Do you want to feel truly empowered from within and progress?

Before we focus on the exercises and strategies for confidence mastery, there is one thing to point out right now.

Nothing in this world works like magic. You may want to get instant results from a remedy, but every approach, every exercise, every technique, and reaching a desired result, takes time. It even takes time for a painkiller to work and relieve your pain. Everything takes time, testing, persistence, and based on the feedback you get from the subsequent result, you will have data to determine if what you're doing is making a difference.

When you fail—and you will—use this as leverage to try something a slightly different way. The only way to not scale up is to give up, or take no action at all. You can only make a difference when you make an effort.

When you are trying to lose weight, you exercise, eat healthily, control your portions, and practice several other measures to get results. and the results take at least 2 to 3 weeks to show up.

Similarly, give confidence-building techniques and approaches time, too. Rewiring your brain to think differently and changing its neuroplasticity takes time and the consistency of practice. It is not an overnight game.

Don't forget the fact that you have been thinking a certain way all your life. Constantly telling yourself day in and day out that you are not good enough and reminiscing your slip-ups has been your go-to thought process all this time. Naturally, this has accustomed your brain to thinking a certain way.

You are not your failures, but rather, learn from the failings on the way and recognize that the result you are striving for can only be reached through a system of trial and error.

Now, to think differently and move from having barely any confidence to scaling up 100X, you need to give yourself and your brain time. The exercises discussed in this guide work and show their magic, but that will require time, effort and testing. It is best to continue practicing them, believing in them, and being patient with them—and yourself—during this process. I understand this is hard work in itself because patience demands great patience. Waiting for results to show up is hard work, truly!

That said, you have to do this for yourself if you want to see some change in your life. Because this is a personal journey, and only you can bring it about. You cannot expect the exercises to work on their own, neither can you expect someone else to carry them out for you because you need that confidence in **you**.

How to Rewire Your Brain with Behavior Repetition

Now that you know you can change your habits and the process by which you can do so, you can lead your brain towards positive thinking and elevating self-confidence. Keep in mind that by continuously behaving a certain way, you can adopt it as a habit.

Confidence makes you happy with yourself; therefore, it has a positive connotation. Just as you'll feel completely fulfilled after acquiring this habit, you will also have to provide your mind with a cheerful and powerful environment to promote confidence in the first place. For this reason, confidence and a positive mindset go hand in hand.

If I show you a painting and ask you to find me six faults in it, I know you will pinpoint all six of them—if not more. Similarly, if I show the same painting to another person with instructions to find six elements of perfection in it, certain things will come up. Like every painting has flaws and attributes of great finesse, your life is a piece of art, and you are the master artisan of your own life.

Life depends on the type of questions you ask yourself. If it's about focusing on the negative aspects, then your life will be like a gloomy portrait. It would rather be an endearing one if the question were presented the other way around.

Always remember that it's your painting, and only you can ensure your canvas holds a great artwork full of wholesomeness, delight, mystery and creative ambition. To make your drawing shine, you need to intensify your light.

The implication here is that everything depends on your perspective in life and the belief system behind your approach. The first step towards this lovely journey is to develop a positive mindset and promote constructive thinking by expanding on your ideas.

Question everything you don't know and analyze everything you claim to know. Confidence is a journey of growth and, when you make it your mission to learn and achieve fulfillment through self-discovery, your confidence takes on a life of its own.

Seek Gratitude

If you keep looking for problems in your life, you will always find them. If you stop complaining and start being grateful for your blessings, you will find yourself expressing gratitude all the time. Life will start to throw random surprises at you, and you will rarely find any issues because your mind will be too busy counting your bounties.

Once you start practicing this, it will only be a matter of time until you completely acquire it as a habit. Consistency is the key to building the habit, so make sure to engage in it daily.

After attaining mental relaxation, the next step is to reform your confidence. To rewire your brain to upgrade your confidence, start working on the following tips:

- ☐ Suppose you go out in a social setting feeling uncomfortable, and you want to change this trait.

- ☐ A good pointer is to start viewing yourself from the eyes of others around you in your mind. This way, you will immediately get to know how you are acting, and it is visible. You will instantly start to exert your influence and will try to portray assertiveness. This is a good tip to initiate the process.

- ☐ Don't stop; keep going. In some time, it'll start gradually becoming effortless. Eventually, you will manage to suppress your self-consciousness. This was just one example; there could be numerous instances where you need to be confident. The rule is simple: try taking baby steps towards it, slowly increasing the magnitude, and challenge yourself to ace it.

An important aspect of confidence is **visual confidence**. Let us get some insight into what this is.

Visual Confidence

We all see movies and are aware of how powerful and vigorous personalities inspire us. We all have almost the same impression of a perfect-looking person in our minds. We have this image because we have seen such people and their lifestyles in movies or have read about them in books and stories.

Yes, you can make this your reality by actively imagining yourself carrying out these roles, by feeling how you will act once you become the person of your dreams, and most importantly, accepting that it is achievable.

How you feel while visualizing all the perfect scenarios in mind is called visual confidence. The way it gives you butterflies in your stomach, and you start to become impatient with excitement. In other words, building confidence by envisaging it is visual confidence.

After developing an idea of what it takes to look like a strong and glamorous person, you will automatically begin to quit negative behaviors. Instead, you will try to form new and positive ones. You will start working on achieving that physical existence because you already possess that aptitude. This newly built inclination will serve as a motivational source that propels your capacity and willingness to keep moving forward in life.

5 Repetitive Positive Behaviors to Redirect Negative Confidence

Have you ever wondered if there's one thing that causes people to be successful and whether this is the same factor that stands between you and achieving all your goals? Would you like to know what this element is and how it affects you?

The answer is **positive confidence.**

We consider a greater level of self-confidence "positive confidence" and a lower level of confidence "negative confidence." If you have more confidence, you'll be well on your way to conquest; on the other hand, you would stall somewhere along the way if you have less confidence—or negative confidence. Therefore, the key to growth is "positive confidence."

Negative confidence hinders the self-development process. It lets you down every time and makes you believe that your endeavors are worthless. If you have low self-esteem, you often feel de-energized and demotivated. Don't worry, it's controllable, which is why we are here: to pull you out of it!

There are some helpful tips you can use to change your negative confidence into a positive one. These tips are practical and easily integrated into your daily routine. If you add them to your daily habit stack, I can assure you that you will become unstoppable.

Below is a list of five behaviors that can assist you in promoting positive confidence. Let us tackle them one by one to empower you with wisdom that can help you pave the way for greatness:

VISUALIZATION SESSION

Visualization is like a relaxing exercise where you picture an experience in your mind before actually acting on it. As a result, you trick your brain into believing that whatever you are imagining is real. Visualization is a powerful tool you can use to meet your aspirations and achieve all sorts of goals in life.

The 5 best advantages of practicing visualization are listed here:

1. **Visualization increases your epic performance**: You conduct yourself with ease and grace when you're living the life of your dreams. This is because you are well-acquainted with achieving your goals. In other words, you are familiar with how success feels.

2. **Visualization increases your focus**: When you use your mind to imagine different possibilities of a winning streak, you form new neural connections. This helps you concentrate better when exposed to such stimuli later in life.

3. **Visualization strengthens your courage**: Seeing yourself past those hurdles makes you believe in your capabilities. You become convinced to take this journey and move towards a better "you."

4. **Visualization decreases stress and anxiety**: As you are well-acquainted with the roles you play after becoming confident, it doesn't scare you when it all happens in real life. You stay in your position. You know you have got this, and you will accomplish your goals, so you keep powering through despite the obstacles that come your way.

5. **Visualization relieves insomnia by relaxing your senses**: Studies show that regular visualization helps you sleep better and fight sleep problems such as insomnia. This is because visualization creates a calming effect in your brain, keeping it from racing. As a result, your mind can easily shut off while you lie down to sleep.

Imagine how differently you would act in your daily routine once you upgrade your confidence. The best thing about visualization is that it covers more than one domain of your personality.

Besides focusing on making you comfortable with pursuing your desires, it also helps you distress, sleep properly, and perform better at the same time. Therefore, visualization increases your capacity to go after your life objectives with ease, health, and determination.

Now that you know the power of visualization, here is how you put it into action:

1. Find yourself a quiet space and get into a comfortable sitting position.

2. Put on your headphones and play your best inspirational music. Listening to a song with a slow rhythm allows you to tune in and focus better. I suggest Weightless by Marconi Union.

3. Close your eyes and take three full breaths. Focusing in on your breathing will help to clear your mind of chaos. Breathe in deeply from your diaphragm, pushing out your stomach, and inhaling for 3-4 seconds. Now exhale for 4 seconds. Continue this practice as you put your vision to work.

4. **Think about all the ways you can be prolific.** This might be delivering public speeches, hosting a big office event, conducting high-end meetings, being perfect at what you do, bringing up new ideas and proposing them to your boss, volunteering for live work presentations to clients and investors. Try to feel everything related to the scenario you're visualizing. With a lot of determination, you can achieve all of this and more.

5. **Think of a scenario where you would like to feel incredibly confident.** Now visualize yourself coming off as the strongest, most confident figure in the scene. For example, you could see yourself addressing a crowd of 200 people, all of them listening intently to every word you say.

6. Add details to the visualization by imagining more sights, colors, sounds, expressions, and the likes. For example, if you're visualizing yourself speaking to a large crowd of people about justice and equality, or any other topic, think of the color of your attire, the sounds you hear, the uproar of the audience, the lights on the stage, and other details.

   The more you concentrate on visualizing the details, the more alive the entire scenario becomes in your mind—and thus, the more impactful it is. This practice engages you better in the experience that ultimately helps you inject more belief in it. The more you believe it, the more confident you feel.

7. Random thoughts will disrupt your session, but don't let them stop you. Retake the same initial steps to regain that meditative state.

8. A ten to fifteen-minute exercise would be sufficient, so try to stick to this time duration at the start. If it feels too much, begin with just 5 minutes and slowly increase the duration of the practice.

In addition, work on the following:

- Every night before going to sleep, close your eyes for ten minutes and visualize that you are playing such a role in your current life.

- Imagine how differently you would act in your daily routine.

- Think and feel about doing things you normally feel scared of.

- Doing this ten-minute exercise every day is a good way to indulge in behavior repetition. This way, new neuronal connections will form and will be strengthened further by regular practice.

- Once you have set a good strong network of interconnecting neurons, all of it will start coming to you naturally.

Making this a part of your routine is a good way to indulge in behavior repetition. This way, new synapses or neural links will form, strengthening the pathway further. Once you have set a good strong network of interconnecting neurons, all of it will start to come naturally to you.

As you work on this behavior, you need to start working on another practice.

CREATE A MISSION STATEMENT

Have you ever seen mission statements on the walls when you walk into some organization or a company? These define the identity and purpose of an organization. Mission statements set objectives and an approach to reach those objectives. In other words, it helps fulfill the organization's primary goals, allowing it to move towards its vision.

A vision statement, on the other hand, is generic. It reflects the company's ultimate aim, unrestricted by a specific product line or service.

Like other businesses, you can also set a mission statement for yourself, marking your ambitions and targets. A personal mission statement helps you recognize who you are, what you aspire to be, and how to pursue it with motivation.

Confidence is a collective name for your vocations and various pursuits in life. The expression is incomplete if you say that becoming confident is your goal. Why do you want to become confident? What will you do once you are confident? Who do you want to become by achieving confidence?

Confidence is an important asset that helps you proceed towards your targets in life. Therefore, unlocking this level would mean you have unlocked all the levels, or the whole game of your life.

A personal mission statement helps you in several ways:

- Outlines the essential features of your "WHY": A personal mission statement asks you to sit down and think about what "you" want to become and contribute to the world. It lets you define your desires and adds meaning to your life. You feel like you have an identity and, don't have to follow what people and society expect you to do.

- ☐ When you put your wishes and dreams into writing and hang it in your room, it motivates and inspires you to keep going every time you look at them.

- ☐ Keeps you focused: A mission statement reminds you of your purpose every time you look at it. It allows you to maintain your focus during life's many ups and downs and encourages you to keep going.

- ☐ Your mind easily and quickly wanders away into other thoughts and objectives; having a mission statement hung somewhere near you helps keep your primary goal in mind. With a bigger picture in mind, you would get up and start planning to get there.

- ☐ Simplifies decision-taking: A personal mission statement lets you see the bigger picture, making it easier to make the tough calls. Knowing what you want makes it easy to choose options that align with the person you want to become. Once you set a mission for yourself, the choice becomes easier.

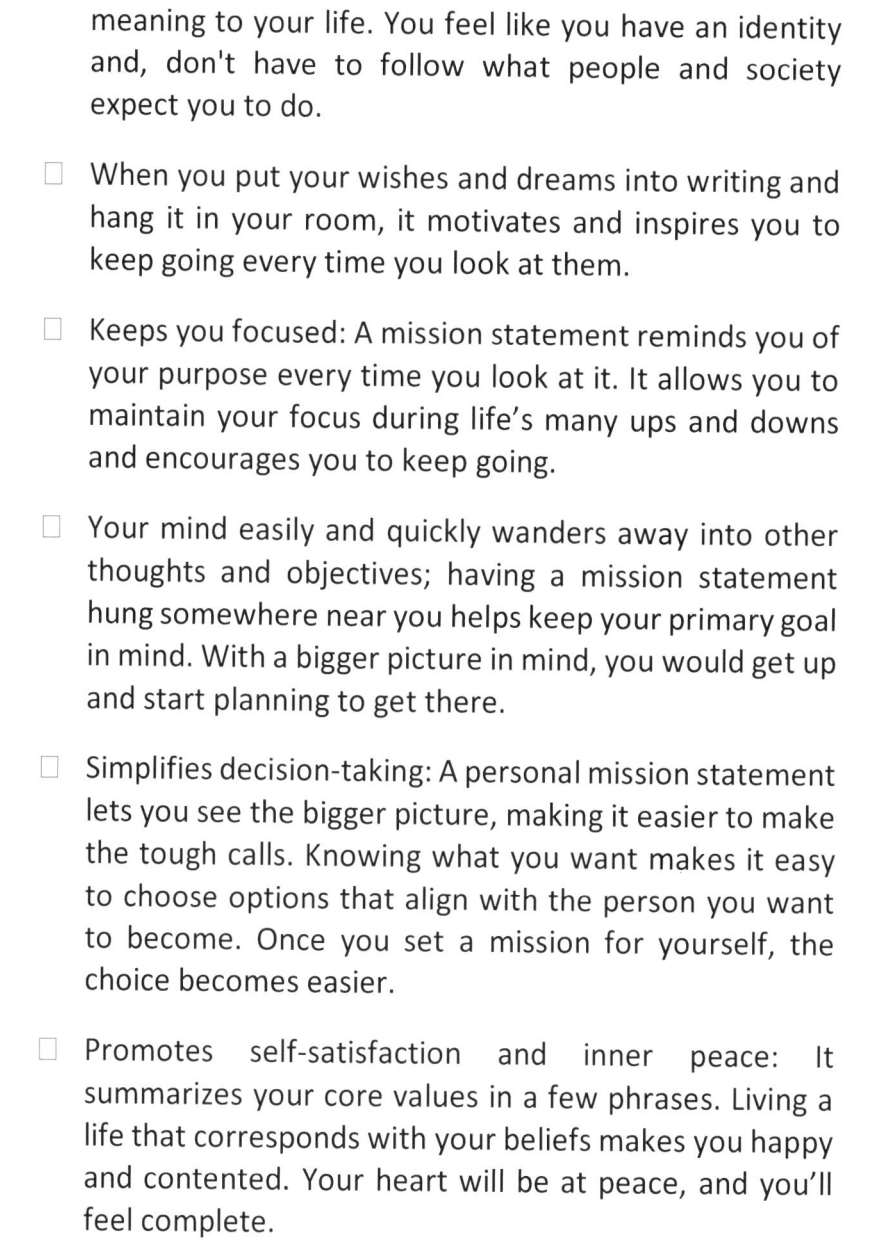

- ☐ Promotes self-satisfaction and inner peace: It summarizes your core values in a few phrases. Living a life that corresponds with your beliefs makes you happy and contented. Your heart will be at peace, and you'll feel complete.

A mission statement lets you decide which reality you want, and guides you as you work towards actualizing this reality.

Many people live their lives based on family or societal expectations of what it means to be a notable personality.

Carrying out such healthy activities would divert your mind from thinking that you are worthless and lacking the confidence to believe in your potential and actively chase your dreams and wishes.

Just writing a mission statement would be very thought-provoking for you; it might even change your entire personal outlook—mostly about yourself. This could be your first step towards becoming the star of your league.

How to write a mission statement

Use the guidelines to write your mission statement:

- Write down what you know about yourself

- Think of what you are passionate about and want to become in your life–try thinking of what you can contribute to the world

- Jot down what's important to you. It could be anything or anyone.

- Next, think of your most important aims in life regarding academic performance, work, career, health, and relationships–try applying exploration tools for this—like what, why, when, where, and how.

- Get feedback from your colleagues, teachers, and managers–what they think best suits you or what you're good at doing.

- ☐ Be true to yourself and make amendments to it as you grow, and your goals change.

- ☐ Restrict your mission statement to 1-2 statements—try to develop one complete sentence. For example, you could try writing down words that describe you and bring them to a shortlist of one word. Give points to each factor on a scale of importance and value it adds to your life to help you get started.

- ☐ Reflect on your purpose in this life. What do you think you are meant to do and would always want to be involved in? Once you figure out your passions, potentials, skills, ambitions, and the aspects you have been thinking about before, think of what truly brings you value and meaning. Explore those areas and write them down.

Remember that your mission statement has to be something that connects all these dots. For instance, you may realize you have a knack for writing, and you want to educate people through your books and create your legacy in the field. That could be your purpose in life, and your mission statement must revolve around that too.

When curating your mission statement, it is best to focus on the mission and do your best to describe it concisely without making it sound abrupt and meaningless. For instance, you could say, "To become a notable writer in the field of personal improvement so I can help people improve their lives." This very concise, precise, and meaningful mission statement clearly points out what you aspire to do.

On the other hand, statements such as, "To become a writer who gives people value," or "to write, so people feel good about themselves" sound vague and incomplete. They describe what you want to do, but not clearly, and aren't inspiring too. To ensure you don't make the same mistake, spend some time figuring out your mission and describing it in detail.

This is a very healthy initiative you can take towards bettering yourself. Doing this will also give your mind a break from negative feelings of doubt and fear of disapproval. It's a good way to explore yourself and devise a path based on your aspirations and ambition.

Once you have your mission statement ready, you know what you need to do. After that, you can start taking action to materialize your mission. Your mission statement would not come true by itself, right? You have to take conscious action towards it, which is where intentional action comes in handy.

Take Intentional Action

Intentional action is the process by which you achieve the desired goal. It operates on the belief that the course of action will fulfill a need or longing. An intentional action consists of "action planning" and "strategies" that lead you towards your target.

No, action planning and strategy are not interchangeable; the two have entirely different meanings. An action plan consists of details and steps required to accomplish a goal. It answers questions like what, why, where, when, and how.

A strategy is larger than an action plan. It plans for the future and defines how to execute steps of an action plan in the best possible way.

While devising a strategy, you must consider different aspects and look at the situation as a whole. The purpose of a strategy is to consume time and resources efficiently and effectively.

Taking an intentional action on your mission statement is physically moving towards your aims; You are making an intentional plan to implement and execute action towards your dreams. People often develop inspiring personal mission statements but fail to work on them because they lack guidance. Don't worry; I will run you through the entire plan.

How to create an intentional action plan

1. To take intentional action, you first need to set a target.

2. Make sure you set SMART goals. SMART is an acronym for specific, measurable, attainable, relevant, and time-bound.

3. Make your goal specific by answering the questions: "what do I want to achieve?" "Which restrictions and resources are involved?" "Why is it important?" "Where is it located?" "When do I have to deliver it?" Otherwise, with an unclear goal, you will lose your motivation during the action.

4. Make it measurable by questioning yourself. For example, ask yourself, "how much do I need? "When will I know I have achieved my goal? Asking yourself

such questions gives you a sense of completion and task identification.

5. Having an attainable goal helps you identify your untapped potential and which of your previously neglected opportunities you can use to accomplish your target. Ask yourself questions like, "how can I achieve this goal?" "How realistic is it financially?"

6. A relevant goal would give an impression that it is worthwhile, and you are the right person to work on this goal because it aligns with your values and aspirations, the timing is right, etc. These measures help you evaluate your goals, which ensures that you only set relevant goals. Setting such a goal is critical because you need to have control over it to proceed forward.

7. A time-bound goal allows you to use your time productively. This way, you won't take ages to get past a simple sub-task. Considering questions like, how much can I do in six months, in two weeks, or a day would help you deal with it.

Once your goal is clear, the next step is to design an action plan, which you can do as follows:

1. Make a list the required steps. Don't skip anything, even if you think it is unimportant.

2. Prioritize them and assign realistic deadlines to each task. You can arrange them in order by giving marks to every function.

3. Set milestones. As you decide which magnitude and timeframe to attach to tasks, start from the final step

and work your way up. Suppose your goal is to host an event for 1000 people, but you can only do so comfortably in front of 20 people right now. In that case, your milestones would be about gradually raising the number of individuals and the duration until you can get to that number, which means you would also need to keep practicing in order to master the skill.

4. Plan and gather your resources. Do your best to have everything at hand before you start attempting to achieve anything. Resources could be your budget, electronic gadgets, or people, to name a few

5. Formulate a chart with columns to track your progress. This could be a table, Gantt chart, or a flowchart. Make sure it has easy access and should be editable

After making a complete action plan, the next step is to make a strategy, which you can design as follows:

1. Firstly, be clear about what you value most in your life. The first few things that come to mind are family, health, and career. Think about hidden aims like playing managerial roles, promotion to a higher rank, delivering seminars, hosting big events, motivational speeches, wealth, experience, and personal growth.

2. Conduct personal SWOT. Think about your strengths, weakness, opportunities, and threats. Don't just come up with a self-evaluation; consider getting feedback from others. They could be your family, friends, boss, colleagues, and mentors.

3. Once you know about your strengths and opportunities, try using them effectively to have an edge or selective advantage when implementing your action plan.

4. Accept your weaknesses and consider your threats. Be welcoming and open towards taking negative feedback.

5. Similarly, refrain from using your weaknesses to execute anything.

Creating an intentional action plan and implementing it can be transformative. Some changes would be abrupt, while some might take a little longer. Be patient and consistent with your work.

Whenever you don't feel like following your plan, glance at your mission statement to feel encouraged to keep going. Another good way is to treat and give yourself small rewards for achieving a task successfully, but don't quit. You've come so far; it's just a matter of time and determination before you can fulfill your deepest desires.

Constantly Motivate Yourself with Positive Self-Talk

"Loving or hating the life you are living is solely all in your repeated self-talk." — **Edward Mbiaka**

Each of us has a constant dialogue with ourselves that runs throughout the day. Be it personal commentary, thoughts on your whereabouts during the day, philosophies about life, interpretations of experiences, or any thoughts you have during the day, we all engage in self-talk.

This self-talk usually has a tone. It tends to range from the spectrum of positive to negative, sometimes stopping on the neutral mark. Its positive and negative tone varies depending on the situation and current experiences. That said, some of us have a habit of speaking to ourselves negatively most of the time.

Perhaps every time you decide to start a business, you shun the idea because the voice in your head keeps telling you how awful an idea that is. Perhaps you think about your past slip-ups whenever you decide to act for a theatrical show, your passion. Unfortunately, since the dialogue in your head always keeps you from doing so, you quit pursuing the idea.

Thoughts such as, 'This is not possible,' 'I am stupid,' 'People will make fun of me,' 'This is far too difficult for me,' 'I don't think this suits me,' 'People will judge me,' and the likes are examples of negative self-talk—that is how it sounds.

It is okay to have such apprehensions and doubts once in a while. Let's face it; all of us feel insecure whenever we try to move past our comfort zone, take up a new challenge, or experiment with something new. Such feelings are quite natural.

However, when we focus on such thoughts and internalize them, they turn into our self-talk. For example, if you fixate on 'I am a failure,' you will focus on this day in and day out. Eventually, it will embed in your subconscious mind and start shaping your thought process. Consequently, it makes you believe you are nothing but a failure, leaving you feeling doomed.

Since you have now kick-started your journey towards a confident life, it is important to break this negative thoughts and self-talk cycle. You have started taking action steps to actualize your mission statement, have you not?

During this process, you will experience some hiccups because none of us is impervious to them—moreover, challenges are part of the success process. They upset the better of us. However, the resilient ones who are passionate about achieving their goals always surpass them with positivity. This time around, you should do the same.

Positive self-talk refers to talking to yourself with compassion, encouragement, respect, and love. For example, when you feel shaky about whether you should do a theater performance, you encourage yourself to pursue your passions.

If you falter and upset your diet plan, you motivate yourself to start again. If you lose a client and feel hopeless, you remind yourself of times you succeeded in your aims, thereby recharging your hope.

That is how positive self-talk keeps you motivated and helps ensure you don't let go of your aspirations. As you keep moving forward, you eventually reach the finish line and feel accomplished. That sense of fulfillment boosts your confidence, allowing you to embark on another exciting journey.

Since now you know how positive self-talk can help you, let us focus on what you can do to turn it into a repetitive behavior.

- ☐ Set a time when you will only pay attention to the nature of the thoughts that pop in your head and the type of emotions the thoughts trigger.

- ☐ Dedicate about 10 minutes of your day to this practice. In that time, think of how you feel about yourself, and write that down.

- ☐ Whatever your thoughts are, and whatever connotation they may have, pen it down. For example, if you feel frustrated, think about what sort of thoughts led to that feeling, and trace it back to the dialogue you had with yourself that brought up the emotions of stress and annoyance.

- ☐ If you feel upset about anything or have troublesome thoughts that bother you repeatedly, focus on that and write it down.

- ☐ Once you have identified the pesky thought and statement, thank yourself for bringing it to your awareness.

- ☐ Say something reassuring such as, 'I accept I feel stressed right now because of the suggestions I have been giving to myself.'

- ☐ Next, take that suggestion, and consciously omit negative words from it, then rephrase it. Take an instance where you thought, 'I am stupid for trying to run another business after three consecutive failures because I am not cut out for this.' You can change it to, 'Even after three failures, I want to give myself another try, and this time around, I will achieve my goals.'

- Now chant this new suggestion a couple of times.

- Notice how you feel. You are likely to feel at least 1 to 5% better, if not more, than before. Next, say the suggestion out loud a few more times.

- Every couple of hours in the day, make time to track your thoughts, filter the negative ones, and swap them with positive thoughts.

- Actively work on this practice through the day, every day.

In a couple of weeks, you will consciously start to talk positively with yourself at all times and even stay calm as you tackle life's adversities. Giving yourself constant positive suggestions gradually builds positive self-talk that multiplies your confidence by manifolds.

Improvise and Grow Better

Your level of confidence improves with time and practice. Believing in yourself once—and resorting to demeaning yourself the rest of the time—does not shape your confidence. For example, addressing a crowd of 50 people once and going dormant for the next decade will eventually make your newfound confidence fade away.

To truly empower your confidence to a point where you feel assured all the time, especially when push comes to shove, you need to learn from your mistakes and experiences, improvise, and focus on becoming better than before.

As this does not seem like repetitive behavior that deflects negative confidence and helps you shape positive confidence right now, let's dig into the matter a bit more deeply to give you better comprehension.

After going through a certain experience, we don't extract what we've learned from it and seldom focus on improvisation. For instance, let us take an example that involves confidence.

Perhaps your boss made you the team leader for an important marketing project. You were to direct the team, prepare the brief, and present the proposal to your higher-ups. You were scared at first, but eventually you gained the confidence to pull it off and gave a good presentation.

However, later on, you did not consider which areas you could improve, and hence, you did not work on your weak body language during the first presentation. Instead, you continued using the same body language in many other meetings to follow.

Unfortunately, because you did not receive the same appreciation you did the first time, you began worrying about what went wrong, not realizing that you received the first applause because it was your first time.

The second time you stood in the board room, your audience expected a bit more from you. The expectations rose even higher the third time, the fourth time, and so on.

Most people ignore weaknesses and shortcomings the first couple of times, but not for good. With expectations set, you need to meet them to continue scaling up.

If you do not focus on improving, you become stagnant, and once you become stagnant, your chances of growth reduce with time. Hence, the right way to keep growing more confident and achieving new heights of growth is to learn from your experiences and mistakes, concentrate more on self-improvement, and keep finding ways to get better because that's how you skyrocket your confidence.

Now, **let's learn the step-by-step process**:

- As you implement your action plan and endeavor to achieve your mission, peg small 'performance review' windows to every step. For example, suppose you are working on setting up a Life Coaching business and decide to make a video to introduce yourself to your target audience. In that case, you need to go through the video later and check for ways to speak even better.

- In the same manner, keep taking action and identify areas of improvement.

- As you do this, keep praising yourself for taking the initiative and working on different tasks. Often, when we look for areas of improvement, we become critical of ourselves. Instead of appreciating ourselves for trying, we focus only on what went wrong and somehow become too self-critical. You need to tame this behavior. Focusing on improvisation means more than just overcoming your visible shortcomings. It also means working on other behaviors that keep you from getting better, like becoming overly critical of yourself.

Sometimes, we let go of the need to improve because this habit of criticizing ourselves for little mistakes demoralizes us. That is why when you start identifying your shortcomings, be nice and kind to yourself. Instead of jumping towards bashing yourself, acknowledge your efforts first and then calmly figure out what you need to eliminate or improve.

- After identifying your shortcomings, figure out how to improve them. Brainstorm ideas and write them down. For example, if you stammer when you speak, maybe take a speech therapy class, take lessons online, or see if the stammering breeds from chronic stress and work on that first.

  Similarly, if you want to be a better trainer but lack confidence because you stand at the 'beginners' skill level right now, you can improve your prowess by enrolling in a relevant program.

- Next, you have to take the plunge. Whatever self-improvement route you have identified, work on it and create a schedule for that area. This way, you will know if you need to devote 60 or 120 minutes to improve your skill as an SEO specialist, what days to work on it, and how to execute it.

  Once you have a schedule, it becomes easier to stick to the tasks and execute them on time. Make taking action a regular thing such that, every day, you work on at least one area of improvement and become a refined version of yourself.

We often perceive our ability to speak in front of others as the only yardstick to measure confidence. How well you can speak and how many people you can address isn't the only means of gauging your self-belief.

Self-belief also depends on how you feel about yourself, how you perform in your job, the endeavors you partake in, whether or not you pursue your ambitions, how you interact with others, whether you react or respond to challenges in life, and other similar aspects.

Once you start engaging in self-improvement practices regularly, you will start feeling more empowered, stronger, and poised because, with time, you will see yourself getting better with each passing day. This will give you a gratifying feeling that will reaffirm your faith in yourself.

Part 4: The Bulletproof Confidence Upgrade

"Self-confidence is a superpower. Once you start to believe in yourself, the magic starts happening."

— **Anonymous**

How to Build, Sustain, and Empower Your Confidence

Nobody has ever had a magic wand or a magical elixir that has brought them immense treasures and pleasures in life. That superpower has always been self-belief and confidence driven by clear and specific goals.

At this point in our learning journey together, I am very confident that you have noted an increase in the development of your inner confidence—especially if you have been taking intentional action. And the prospect of building on what you have learned up to now is where the journey becomes more exciting.

Now that you are ready for the next phase, it is time to reveal the **Confidence Upgrade Blueprint**, featuring 15 strategies that help build, sustain and further empower your confidence.

YOUR BUILT-IN CONFIDENCE BLUEPRINT

Any habit you now have has taken some time to develop fully; you did not acquire that behavior overnight. For example, it probably took months—or years—to build the habit of exercise or writing every day to finish your dream novel. Now, when it's 5am in the morning, and your feet hit the floor, you know you need to go for a workout, or sit down at your desk and begin hammering on the keyboard.

You spent time developing these habits. After strengthening its respective neuronal pathways by engaging in it many times, that behavior became automatic and shifted to autopilot mode. Because it became automatic, now you don't need time to think twice about working out. You just do it. The neuronal pathways related to this particular activity have become strong enough for you to carry it out unconsciously.

To feel confident all the time, such that the attitude transfers become automatic, you need to strengthen its neuronal pathways. You need to engage in different strategies repeatedly to the point where you don't have to think twice before feeling completely self-assured.

As you engage in these practices more and more, you will make them habitual, and eventually, you will start exuding confidence all the time, irrespective of your present situation.

Let's push forward and explore these strategies right now.

"I think that the power is the principle. The principle of moving forward, as though you have the confidence to move forward, eventually gives you confidence when you look back and see what you've done."

— Robert Downey, JR.

Strategy #1: Confidence and Self-Directed Language

Self-directed language refers to managing your language and directing it towards a common goal. It is another name for self-talk.

As we have mentioned several times, how you talk to yourself monumentally influences and shapes your confidence. Your confidence keeps dwindling whenever you keep repeatedly bashing yourself and speaking to your subconscious in that same, negative voice that has become second-nature.

One of the best ways to keep that from happening is to engage in positive self-talk and direct your inner and outer language towards rehabilitating your confidence.

Here is what you need to do to make that happen:

- ☐ Start by saying one positive thing to yourself early morning. When you wake up, say something like, 'Today is a good day, and I will achieve all my targets,' or 'I feel great about myself today, who I am and the character I'm building.'

- ☐ As the day progresses, consciously keep those positive suggestions in your mind and direct them more towards yourself. For example, you could say, 'I look good,' 'I feel positive,' or 'I can sense my confidence building from within.'

- ☐ If you have a slip-up during the day, say you missed the subway or forgot to send an email to your coworker on time, say something reassuring such as, 'It is okay. I only need to be more careful moving forward. But it's totally fine to make mistakes. They will happen.'

- ☐ On doing something nice, appreciate yourself by saying positive things like, 'Good job, you are doing so well.'

- ☐ Keep saying positive and encouraging things to yourself day in and day out; the more you do this, the more confident you shall feel with each passing day.

Remember that it takes time to change and build positive self-directed language; the secret to success—in everything—is to exert consistent effort.

STRATEGY #2: CONFIDENCE AND DEFEATING PROCRASTINATION

We all procrastinate, and it's okay to do so because sometimes, we all feel like doing nothing, perhaps because of feeling tired of our monotonous routine. It's important to give yourself breaks; you deserve them. The problem starts when you make giving yourself undeserved breaks a habit.

Postponing an action, delaying, or putting off activities until the last minute is procrastination. Researchers have often described it as "a form of self-control characterized by an unreasonable delay in activities even though it may have negative consequences."

It is no secret that no matter how well-organized and committed you are, like most people, you may find yourself wasting hours on trivial things, like watching TV, updating your Facebook status, or shopping online when you don't actually need anything. You know you should have spent that time learning or working on your business, but you still ignore your priorities.

This happens because of your desire to resist something that feels imposed on you, often revealed as deadlines or expectations from pressing deadlines or expectations. Thus, you try to escape it and spend your time on comparatively lighter activities, like scrolling down on social media or watching a movie.

Whether you are postponing a project, neglecting household chores or avoiding homework, procrastination can have a profound negative effect on your performance and health.

Don't worry! Procrastination is not always a sign of a serious problem. We all practice it at one point or another—yes, even the most successful people you know. As mentioned earlier, although procrastination is normal, it has negative effects when it becomes habitual.

Before we discuss how to overcome chronic procrastination, let's discuss its core causes:

CAUSES OF PROCRASTINATION

You need to feel motivated to work at a certain time. However, if you often wait until you feel in the right frame of mind to accomplish a task, the chances are that the right time never comes.

You often think that projects will not take as long to complete as they will, which leads to false positives when you believe you still have plenty of time to complete them. Soon, however, you realize that you have wasted a lot of time, and you're not even halfway through. As a result, you start panicking and become unable to utilize the rest of your time productively.

Procrastination has many causes that make you feel like deferring your tasks. Some of the most prominent ones are:

- ☐ Academic-related expectations pressure you to score high grades—this could be because your parents compare you with your peers

- ☐ Depression and poor mental state not allowing you to focus properly

- ☐ Your OCD (Obsessive-Compulsive Disorder) increases the workload

- ☐ Not knowing what you need to do, which happens when you fail to map out your tasks

- ☐ Not knowing how to do something and you don't want to figure it out yourself

- ☐ Thinking you can finish it at the last minute

- ☐ Suspicion of illness makes you subconsciously think that you won't manage to do it. As a result, you convince yourself not to take the first step

- ☐ Delaying one task to work on another

HOW PROCRASTINATION AFFECTS CONFIDENCE:

Procrastination causes you to lose valuable time, lowers the quality of your work, and makes you begin feeling bad at the end of the day—because of failing to achieve anything worthwhile. Such feelings make you feel bad about yourself, and your self-esteem takes a hit. It is normal for human beings to procrastinate every once in a while, but letting this habit become chronic can have far-reaching effects on your confidence.

How to beat procrastination

Here are some tips you can use to build boundaries and set priorities, thereby beating procrastination:

1. Recognize and respond to Internal Criticism

2. Observe your speech. Examine yourself when using excuses such as, "I have to do…" or if you permit yourself to fail by saying, "I will try…."

3. Define a plan of action. You are more likely to procrastinate if you don't have an idea or a set plan to achieve your goals. You can make a table listing with all your pending tasks on one column, and their respective stages on the other. Monitor your progress daily and push yourself to check them off your list.

4. Avoid distractions by setting deadlines and taking due breaks once in a while.

5. Reward yourself for your achievements and also hold yourself accountable for failures and learn from them. A self-treat could be a spa day or a shopping trip.

Strategy #3: Confidence and Giving to Others

"If you light a lamp for somebody, it will also brighten your path." — **Buddha**

People who donate their time and effort to others or something they care about have higher self-esteem and general well-being. The question is: how does helping others improve your self-confidence?

Helping others develops self-confidence by changing your brain

When helping others in need, the mesolimbic system, the part of the brain responsible for feelings of reward and happiness, is active. This releases feel-good hormones and neurotransmitters.

Helping others profoundly affects your brain; for example, it enhances happiness and redirects you to a sense of purpose, even if you are facing a challenging situation in life.

It doesn't necessarily mean you have to aid others financially. Even simple things, like a slight gesture of respect, offering your seat to a pregnant woman or a physically impaired person, letting older people enter a room first, carrying someone else's groceries in a train, or helping older people when they are struggling are all top contenders for kind acts.

How to help others and improve your self-confidence

Make a list of your skills, abilities, and experience, and consider how you can serve people using with qualities. Consider the following questions:

- How much time should I devote to helping others?

- What skills do I have that can benefit nonprofits or the community?

- Do I have the resources to donate money?

- Do I have things I don't need that can help someone else?

- Do I love animals, children, help the elderly?

Strategy #4: Confidence and Body Language

Have you ever wondered how some people are so persuasive and dominant over other people in a room? How their energy or charisma attracts everyone's attention? How is every person willing to listen to them and cooperate with anything they propose? Well, effective and influential body language is the game-changer here.

Body language plays a huge role in communicating your confidence in a social setting. Confident people tend to stand upright, have an open stance, look self-assured, and ultimately project a presence of determination and strong will.

On the other hand, people with low self-esteem tend to slouch, cross their arms, or avoid eye contact as defense postures. Various studies indicate that getting used to a "confident posture" can promote your self-esteem and sense of self-worth.

In her book *The Essentials of Business Etiquette*, Barbara Patcher puts it very beautifully by stating: "You control the [message] you send." "I believe that if you present a confident, credible, well-structured image, people will respond to you as if you were all that. Who cares about how you feel inside?" This passage shows that confidence has a lot to do with your capacity to present yourself confidently—and present your message well.

The thing to learn here is to conduct yourself like an assertive person and acquire the art of appearing like one.

How to upgrade your body language

#1: Maintain a firm stand

An effective strategy for building self-esteem is maintaining a strong posture that makes you appear balanced and assured.

When standing, keep your feet firmly planted on the floor, shoulder wide apart and open, and spread your weight evenly on both legs. Try to keep your feet out of the way of the other person to show that you are open to their ideas and opinions.

"This is a state of resilience," Pachter explains in his book. "It's a situation that conveys confidence, not insecurity. You're open to the person you're talking to. And you can stand tall, no matter how tall you are."

Avoid standing in a "humble position" with your legs crossed, arms folded in front of you, or the weight pressed down on one hip.

If your work requires that you sit in a chair for most of the day, practice good posture while sitting, back straight to the chair, and feet firmly planted on the floor. By adopting this position, you should be able to stand upright without leaning forward.

In addition, good posture opens up your airways, thereby ensuring proper breathing.

#2: Posture

In her TED talk on body language, Amy Cuddy, a body language researcher, says that our body energies, many of which include open space positions, can send signals to the brain that make you feel confident. Then, the brain produces more testosterone and lowers your cortisol levels, also called the stress hormone.

Cuddy writes that, when your body mimics the movements of a powerful person, your brain begins to believe that you have power. She further notes that this mental stimulus affects the body, allowing you to skip any negative speech and unproductive thought patterns that can affect you mentally.

Therefore, the more you learn to improve your body language, the easier it gets to adopt confident body language because your body will produce higher testosterone levels.

STRATEGY #5: CONFIDENCE AND DEVELOPING BETTER HABITS

Scientific research has proven that confident people are more financially successful and wealthier in their lives than those who lack confidence. Unfortunately, many of us forget that confidence can also come from building healthier and more positive habits.

Confident people have **habits** that differ greatly from the habits of those who struggle with building confidence.

Therefore, to empower yourself and your confidence, you also need to build habits conducive to skyrocketing your confidence.

Here are the habits:

Asking for help

Many of us often struggle with asking someone for help. We fear that not knowing everything may have some backlash, which keeps us from asking for help and support, consequently hindering our growth.

In contrast, confident people have no issue with not being Mr./Ms. Know It All. They know they cannot know everything; hence, whenever they struggle with something, they openly ask for help on the matter.

To become more self-confident, you need to have the same attitude. It is good to increase your knowledge and skill level, but if you require support in any area, go ahead and ask for it, preferably from an expert.

Create your happiness

Insecure people have a constant need to seek validation from others to feel good. On the other hand, confident folks create their own happiness by appreciating themselves and not caring about what or how others feel about them.

This is a difficult habit to nurture but an important one. Once you stop associating your happiness with external validation, you feel liberated and independent, able to enjoy your life fully.

To build this habit, start doing the following:

- Whenever you **achieve a milestone or goal**, appreciate yourself, reward yourself for the great work done, and then move on.
- **Announce** only the most monumental updates in your life to others because broadcasting every milestone makes you crave external attention and validation.
- **Curate a list of things and activities that make you happy** and engage in them every day. For instance, you could paint one day, watch movies the other day, go for a walk the next day, and so on. Doing this will help ensure that you do something that brings you happiness and leaves you feeling good about yourself, slowly decreasing your dependence on others for your sense of worth and happiness.

Take Risks

Confident people believe that if they don't take a certain risk now, they are likely to regret not pursuing it later. They also understand that calculated risks often come with great rewards, and thus, they are more willing to take these risks.

That said, confident people don't jump to the gun; they only take calculated risks. To take charge of your life, you need to start doing the same. Whenever you feel like doing something or are in a situation where you have the option of taking the risk, analyze the risk.

Assess the pros and cons associated with it. Think of what may or may not happen if you don't take that plunge. Consider the value you will get by taking that risk. Once you have made that analysis, take that risk.

Taking risks feels tough at first, but once you start and keep taking risks, you will soon get the hang of it, and it will stop seeming abnormal, difficult, or threatening then.

Celebrate others (and their success)

Confident folks know life isn't a rat race. They know their worth and that of others, which is why appreciating others comes easily to them.

In addition, they let go of the need to judge others because they know that judging others only defines them. Confidence eliminates the need to prove yourself to others or judge them because you know your worth.

This realization allows you to have a big heart and makes you comfortable around other successful people because you learn how to celebrate their successes. To start being that kind of an individual, here's what you should do:

Every time an acquaintance, a loved one, a coworker, or anybody you know accomplishes something, offer wholeheartedly praise. Shun judgments that pop into your mind and instead, shower the person with genuine appreciation.

Each time you have judgmental thoughts about another person, think about this: we all have our flaws. Shake off that judgment and think of something good about that person. A friend of mine once told me, "I make eliminating judgments easy—you just like everybody without criticism or overthinking. I just make a decision to like everybody, and life becomes so much easier."

Make a list of your strengths and accomplishments, and go through them for a few minutes every morning. This exercise boosts your self-belief, makes you reaffirm your sense of worth, and keeps you from being envious of the success of those around you.

As you start working on these habits, you attain a newfound sense of confidence that only grows stronger with time.

Strategy #6: Confidence and Taking Control of Your Day

Many of us are unproductive because we spend more time on meetings and emails instead of working on our targets. Many others fail to achieve progress because of failing to complete the right work or burning out because we cannot deal with the pressure of the immense workload.

All these problems boil down to an inadequate capacity to take control of our day and time. If you allow external factors to control your day or get carried away with routine interruptions, you usually lose control over your time, day, and life in general. This needs to stop if you are to become confident and successful in your life and work.

When you control your time and day, you know what, when, why, and how you need to do something. This makes it easier to infuse a smoother order into your routine. Consequently, you accomplish your targets and feel confident.

Here's what you need to do:

Plan your day

Always create a monthly plan based on your goals. Divide that plans into weekly plans for the four weeks of the month. For each weekly plan, know what you need to get done in that week.

In addition, go through the next day's plan the night before to ensure you know what you need to do the following day, making it easier to manage contingencies timely and ensure you don't get carried away with unimportant stuff.

Know your priorities

Make an effort to figure out your genuine priorities. Once you know your high-priority tasks that directly boost your productivity, put them first on the schedule.

Block in 2 hours of the day for high priority tasks

Dedicate at least 2 hours of your day to your most pressing tasks—all the major activities that directly impact your targets. It does not take us much time to do what we want, but distractions keep us from doing the important tasks.

Scrolling down your social media newsfeed, random browsing, daydreaming, chatting with friends, and simply being lazy are some of the distractions around us. We keep trying to do everything, all at once, and often get nothing done even after 24 hours, or 16 hours, if we set aside 8 hours for sleep and rest.

If we set aside a minimum of 2 hours of the day for our important tasks and engage in them and nothing else, we would start getting our work done. You will be surprised to see how you can complete many of your tasks in half the time you usually spend on your chores otherwise.

Group similar tasks

If you have two or more related tasks, batch them together instead of tending to them individually. For instance, you can create many videos in one go and schedule them to upload at intervals. Instead of replying to every email individually, set aside 40 minutes to check and respond to important emails. When you group relevant tasks, you spend less time on them, which improves your efficiency.

Begin tasks with intention

Start with an intention when you are about to work on an activity. This means you should think of the task and write down what you are about to do, why it matters, and how to do it. This simple technique clarifies any ambiguities related to the task, allowing you to focus on it well and do it successfully.

After clarifying what you need to do, start working on it right away. Plan and organize your days to infuse structure in your life.

Strategy #7: Confidence and Your Emotional States

Your emotional states also hugely affect your confidence. Therefore, to feel self-confident, it is crucial to keep your emotions in check and not allow them to overpower your ability to think and act rationally.

First and foremost, understand that all emotions are just emotions. The adjectives of good or bad that we assign to our emotions have everything to do with how we react or respond to our emotions. For example, reacting to your anger by throwing things at a friend makes the anger 'bad.' If you don't lash out in anger, your anger will dissipate on its own.

Every time you feel an emotion, sit with it and let it cool down by taking deep breaths. Inhale to a count of 5 through your nose, and exhale to a count of 7 through your mouth.

Work on this practice every time you experience an intense emotion—joy, sadness, envy, or jealousy.

When it calms down, think of what you should do. We call this responding, and when you respond instead of reacting to an emotion, you make informed decisions that empower your confidence.

Naturally, it will take time to master this strategy, but if you keep working on it, you will reach a point where you don't allow your emotions to sabotage your self-belief.

Strategy #8: Confidence and Resolving Regret, Blame and Shame

Have you found yourself wishing you hadn't worked on a task, or maybe you had done something instead of nothing? That is a relatable example of regret.

Unfortunately, it doesn't stop there. Regret often makes us spiral into other negatively impacting emotions like shame. To hide our shame, we look for someone to blame.

I'm pretty sure you are wondering how these emotions connect to confidence. Well, the answer is simple.

How do these make you feel? Regret makes you question yourself and your judgment. It makes you judge yourself more cruelly, and you end up in a brutal cycle of self-loathing.

On the other hand, shame makes you think you aren't good enough. It leads you to feel inferior to others and makes you lower your standards.

Finally, blame triggers a fight response to the feeling of shame. However, this response is neither beneficial nor productive. It makes you avoid responsibility, thereby hindering self-growth. These emotions often lead to self-fulfilling prophecies. Thus, you end up doing more things you later regret, and your confidence takes a major hit.

Now that you have established how you feel, it's important to know how to overcome these emotions and use them to enhance your confidence.

Here's what I suggest you do.

Process your emotions

The first step to overcoming any problem is to accept the problem. Similarly, you must first acknowledge and accept your emotions. One way to do this is to say how you feel out loud or write down your feelings. Jot down everything, from how you feel to what you have learned.

Regulate your inner critic

It can be challenging to counter the negative voices in our head, but we must control them and stop reliving the negative moments. Whenever you notice yourself being overly critical, take a piece of paper and write all the unpleasant things that come to mind.

Then, flip the page over, and for every negative word or sentence, write a positive one. This exercise helps you put things into perspective and starts you on your self-healing journey.

Change your perspective

Accept the fact that you are human, and humans make mistakes. Instead of feeling discouraged by your mistakes, view them as an opportunity to learn and grow. Life is a culmination of experiences, and every event teaches you something—but you have to be willing to see it.

Forgive yourself

The best way to let things go and move on is by forgiving yourself. We remember to treat others with understanding and care, but we forget that we owe ourselves the same. We are also living creatures, and living creatures thrive best in a positive environment.

Forgiving yourself is not easy; hence, take your time, but don't forget that you deserve forgiveness too.

Incorporate these techniques into your daily routine to start making a difference.

"Inaction breeds doubt and fear. Action breeds confidence and courage. If you want to conquer fear, do not sit home and think about it. Go out and get busy."

— **Dale Carnegie**

Strategy #9: Confidence and Strategic Decision Making

Strategic decision-making is beneficial to everyone on a professional and personal level. Strategic decision-making means viewing the bigger picture and making decisions that will help you effectively achieve your goals.

Although it seems common sense, many people struggle to implement this in their daily lives. Strategic decision-making can help you reach your goals quicker, make fewer mistakes and boost your self-confidence.

Strategic Decision Making has five simple steps:

1. Recognize the problem or task and gather facts
2. Think of other viable solutions and weigh them against each other
3. Choose the best one
4. Implement the decision
5. Review the results and make changes accordingly

These steps may seem daunting at first, but you can tackle the problem easily by keeping in mind the following tips:

Don't assume you know everything

Always take time to understand the situation by releasing control. When you accept that you don't have all the answers, you allow yourself to seek the truth sooner.

Not everything is as it appears

Save your judgment for when you have all the facts. In the beginning, some decisions seem more desirable than others, but you will soon see that as you start to gather facts, the once-attractive offer can quickly turn ugly.

To make sure your biases do not interfere with your decision-making, write down all your thoughts about a viable option on a paper. Doing this will help you identify and remember your biases and help you remain objective.

Think outside the box

Create multiple scenarios that help you prepare for all possible outcomes. Discuss your idea or decision with your friends or colleagues in brainstorming sessions. Allow everyone to speak their mind freely and without judgment. This will help you feel more confident about your decisions, and you will feel better about taking responsibility for the results, either positive or negative.

Start following these guidelines, be confident, and allow yourself to understand that there is no perfect solution. Have the ability to reevaluate your decisions. Do not feel ashamed if the outcome is not the one you wanted. You can change or fix most things. This displays your confidence in your decisions and helps add to your expertise.

STRATEGY #10: CONFIDENCE AND MONEY

The more money you have, the more confidence you will have, right? That is the general rule everyone usually knows. Most people directly link money to confidence and happiness. But you have heard about people who might be rolling in dollars but still unhappy and unconfident, right?

Does this mean that money and confidence have no relation? Well, not exactly. There is a link.

Most people confuse having money with being rich. These are essentially two different things. Being rich guarantees confidence, while having money does not. A rich person possesses an abundant mindset. Let me elaborate on this:

To transform your physical surroundings, you must first learn to develop your emotional state. Once you understand that money cannot fix everything or make up for your lack of confidence, you will also find yourself a lot richer.

The steps below will start you on your journey to a more abundant mindset:

Acceptance is the key

Understand that money will never make up for your lack of confidence. Accepting this reality can prove challenging, but you can make it easier by talking to friends and family members who have the opposite view of money. Engaging in a healthy debate with those who do not believe money is the solution to everything will help broaden your perspective.

Practice reciting affirmations

You probably know of well-off people—in terms of money—who are unhappy and who always complain about their jobs. What is stopping them from quitting and looking for a new one? It's not money; it's their lack of confidence.

They feel as though they don't have enough to offer. Practicing affirmations is a good way to change that perspective and boost your confidence.

Several examples of affirmations for this include:

- "I can get the job/scholarship/grade I want."
- "Confidence is not the same as money. You can have one without the other."
- "I am in control. I control my mindset and my living expenditure."
- "People trust me enough to depend on me. I should also trust myself."
- "I am grateful for everything I have."

Focus on what you have, not on what you don't have

Once you start practicing gratefulness, the feelings of not having enough money will eventually disappear. Keep a diary and before you go to sleep, list down all the things you are grateful for in various aspects of your life. Habitually practicing this will help shift your focus from the negative aspects of the day to the positives.

Pay attention to the words you use

Though they may seem insignificant, they can have a long-term impact on your mentality. Try to use more neutral or positive words instead of discouraging ones. For example, instead of saying things like, "Sorry for the wait" and "I feel drained/exhausted," say "Thank you for waiting for me" and "I need to rest."

Strategy #11: Confidence and Relationships

As we have seen above, confidence is the answer to most of the problems we face in our daily lives. Relationships are no exceptions.

Confidence helps you to be more open to new relationship possibilities and have potentially wonderful encounters. In addition, working on strengthening your relationships also boosts your confidence. "How," you may ask? You feel cared for and special when you have loved ones around you, which automatically empowers your confidence.

Let me describe some ways to improve your bond with loved ones, and consequently, your confidence.

Know your self-worth

Be confident in your abilities and what you have to offer as a person. Just because your last relationship didn't work out does not mean something is wrong with you. You two were just not meant to be; that is all. Do not let your thoughts spiral out of control and jump to conclusions.

Discuss things with loved ones

If something that happened in the past is still bothering you or you aren't over the last argument you two had, talk to your partner. If you feel that something your partner is doing affects your confidence negatively, communicate it. Tell them what is bothering you and reach a solution together.

Do not discuss relationships with friends who are always talking negatively about the opposite gender: We often make this mistake, leading to paranoia. If you want relationship advice, ask friends who are in successful relationships or those who are neutral. Most importantly, ask for their opinions but do not become dependent on them and do everything they tell you without question. It's your relationship, not theirs. So, trust yourself to make the right decisions.

Set high standards

Not everyone you meet will fit into your life. Only invest in those people who are willing to do the same for you. Having high standards does not mean being uncompromising. It just means compromising for the right people, people who will be there for you when you have nothing to offer or when you are down, those who love and adore you for who you are, not for what you have.

Express your love and care for loved ones

Spend quality time with loved ones to let them know they truly matter to you. Make it a must to express your affection to them, and work on little gestures of love and care such as sending loving messages, surprising them with gifts, and having heart-to-heart talks.

As you work on these particular aspects, you will notice a marked improvement in your relationships and level of self-belief. Embrace that self-confidence and look forward to new opportunities.

Strategy #12: Confidence and Health

People who are in better health have more self-esteem and achieve greater success in life. Confidence and health are inextricably linked; they are mutually reinforcing, and one leads to the other. The question is, what's the connection between health and confidence?

It's tempting to say, "If I were more confident, I'd feel better about myself," but thinking this way is a fallacy or faulty belief. The truth is that if you feel good about yourself and believe in your skills, it will be easier to create and stick to reasonable physical goals. Simultaneously, if you are in good bodily or mental health, it will be easier to feel good about yourself.

The connection is mutual causality: they affect each other; thus, we must improve both to maintain the two.

Deciding to change your life is never simple. Breaking old habits and forming new ones can be difficult and even discouraging at times. It is, nevertheless, not impossible.

To improve your health, you can use the following tips:

- Identify and determine which of your undesirable or unhealthy habits you want to change. For example, if you are physically inactive, consult a doctor before committing yourself to an exercise routine.

- Recognize that it will take time and that you may have setbacks. Make a plan with goals and start small. You don't have to revamp your diet at once. You can begin by eliminating soda from your diet.

Then, one by one, you may begin to eliminate other junk foods and replace them with healthier alternatives.

- [ ] Don't restrict yourself to just one type of diet or activity. It can be discouraging to continue eating the same foods. Thus, make an effort to eat various foods and vary the type and intensity of exercise you do daily or weekly.

- [ ] You don't have to force yourself to eat food you don't like. In this day and age, a little research is all it takes to find food that is both healthy and appealing to you.

- [ ] Hold yourself responsible for making the necessary changes. Don't blame others or a lack of time for your inability to modify unhealthy habits

"A clear vision, backed by definite plans, gives you a tremendous feeling of confidence and personal power."

—Brian Tracy

Strategy #13: Confidence and Life Planning/Organization

Planning and organizing our life gives us the confidence that things are in control. It gives us the courage to take risks that others may be hesitant to take, allowing us to move forward without fear of competition.

We can identify the associated hazards, weigh and categorize them, prioritize them, and develop a reaction strategy by planning. Using this approach, we can turn dangers into opportunities and reap the benefits of doing so.

Life Plan

A life plan is a road map for your life. It helps you prioritize your goals, make decisions based on your priorities, and get closer to the life you desire. While it should give you a clear direction in life, it should also be adaptable. It's your unique roadmap for how you want to live, what matters to you, and what you need to do to get there.

A life plan will make you confident because you will feel in control of your life. To create a life plan you can:

- Look at what's not working. Doing this will help you know what you want to alter in which areas of your life when deciding how to build a life plan.

- To ensure you're spending your time properly, consider what you value most in life and pay attention to how you behave in real-life situations where you express these values in one way or the other.

- [ ] Establish high-level goals for the person you want to be now that you have a concept of the life you desire and what is important in your life. These are the objectives you aim to achieve over some time.

- [ ] Examine your list of "what's not working" and determine the fundamental problems, then get rid of or attenuate whatever is holding you back.

- [ ] Create structures in your life that support the changes you want to see, and then establish a plan of action to get there.

After becoming aware, implement these measures to regain control of your life.

Strategy #14: Confidence and Setting Your Mindset/Attitude

What springs to your mind when you hear the word "confidence"? Most people associate confidence with self-assuredness. Others consider confidence a trait, a conviction in one's skills, or self-esteem. None of these are what confidence truly is.

Confidence is a state of mind, not a sensation. Nervousness, worry, trepidation, and fear are all perfectly acceptable emotions. Confident individuals also experience these things yet remain confident.

People also assume that accomplishments would lead to confidence; that if they did this or achieved that, they would walk around exuding confidence all the time. They believe that there is a threshold beyond which they will no longer struggle with confidence.

Such people may become trapped in a vicious loop of feeling as if they are never doing enough. There is no such point. You'll never be at a point where you'll have it all figured out. You have to train your brain for that.

When you train your brain to cultivate confidence, the challenges you face become a lot more enjoyable, and your successful experiences become even more rewarding. Your brain is a muscle, and like any other muscle, you can train and grow it. If you want to build confidence, you can do so with repetition, a never-say-die attitude, and an intentional approach—because change is never easy.

Confidence is something we choose to invest in; it isn't just something that happens to us.

Exercises to Attain a Mindset of Confidence

- ☐ Take a few moments to write down what makes you unique. Make a list of the things you stand for and what you value.

- ☐ Choose who you want to be and work hard to become that person.

- ☐ When you're feeling down, reach out to someone you admire and remind yourself that it's natural to suffer. Take a few deep breaths, develop a strategy, and keep moving forward.

- ☐ Look at life as an experience rather than a performance.

Confidence is a mindset, not a destination. When you're coming off a rough week or just don't feel confident in yourself, remember that others, even the "confident" ones, have been there before. The more you practice being in that mindset, the more natural it will become.

Strategy #15: Confidence and Approaching Discomfort

As a species, we've evolved to seek comfort and cling to what we know. However, our comfort zones are not where we make life-altering decisions. To do so, we must get comfortable with being uncomfortable.

There is a distinction between what we want and what we need. To varying degrees, we all crave comfort. However, what we require to achieve—our objectives—is in direct conflict with our desire for comfort. Discomfort is where we grow.

You cannot achieve high self-esteem by always staying in your comfort zone. Growth demands that you do things that make you uncomfortable. Often, this entails stepping outside your comfort zone and constantly challenging yourself.

The deeper you push yourself outside your comfort zone, the less certain you are about your ability to succeed in that environment. However, therein lies the opportunity for growth.

If you want to improve your confidence, you must put yourself in difficult situations to prove—mostly to yourself—that you have the talents and traits to succeed. Putting yourself in a position where you can fail—aka taking a risk—is an important part of empowering your self-confidence, and once you've done so, you'll realize how talented you are.

In order for you to push forward, consider these points:

- Realize that unpleasant feelings will pass.

- Build a wall of resistance against discomfort. With every small action you take, your resistance will decrease as you hack away at negative thoughts holding you back.

- Accept discomfort as a necessary part of the learning process.

- Visualize the bigger picture. Think about the long-term gains of self-growth. You want to be a confident person with a healthy self-esteem that attracts the kind of people who love and support you. Taking action now will help you to achieve this.

- Face your fears. To conquer fear, you must confront it, and that takes courage every single day. You must show up and do the work.

- It is critical to set hard, realistic, and attainable goals that are also not overly demanding.

- Ask yourself, "What's the worst that could happen?" and know that no matter what happens, you'll be fine.

Now go out there, face your fears, and learn to tolerate the discomfort that leads to growth and more confidence. As you work on these strategies, track your performance, see where you lack, and work on the areas to become better than the person you were yesterday.

You are only in competition with yourself, and your greatest challenge is to beat yourself at your own game of life. You must beat the self-imposed limitations of your own mind, and replace that negative voice with a new language.

Challenge yourself when you feel yourself slipping back into old patterns. Discomfort is about taking the emotional pain and leaning hard into it. Your mind and body will fight for survival when you're fearful, anxious or nervous. Doing nothing in the moment is easier but you will lose out in the long term.

Building confidence is about challenging your present self with the person you desire to become tomorrow, and next week, and the year after that. Growth is an intentional choice and one that we must make in order to thrive towards greatness.

"Kindness in words creates confidence. Kindness in thinking creates profoundness. Kindness in giving creates love."

— **Lao Tzu**

Conclusion

By now, I am sure you understand that your confidence is yours to own. It entirely depends on your self-belief and how you perceive yourself.

I am hopeful that this book has taught you the many shades of confidence, the many aspects about developing it, along with many actionable techniques that can transform you from someone who lacks self-belief to a self-assured individual who feels capable and in control.

You see, the ball has always been in your court. You have always had all the power to do anything you want. A lack of awareness is the only thing that has kept you from tapping into and using this power for self-betterment. Since you are now aware that you have this power, start using it to empower your confidence and self.

Since this book has many small parts that you can easily delve into, pick any segment that resonates with you and work on the concerned aspect. Using this approach allows you to overcome your most pressing issues and gradually enhance your confidence.

I am genuinely grateful to you for getting this book and taking the time to read and implement what you've learned. Thank you!

I wish you luck in this journey and have unshakeable faith that you will soon build the skills to *Empower Your Confidence,* making this life your best life moving forward.

Scott Allan

"Don't wait until everything is just right. It will never be perfect. There will always be challenges, obstacles and less than perfect conditions. So what? Get started now. With each step you take, you will grow stronger and stronger, more and more skilled, more and more self-confident, and more and more successful."

— Mark Victor Hansen

Empower Your Thoughts (Bonus Chapter #1)

Turn the page to read a chapter from **Empower Your Thoughts**
(Book #2 in the *Pathways to Mastery* series)

Reduce Your Worry Habit

If you observe your own thinking and how your mind interacts with the world, you become a passenger on a wild ride through a theme park. You can be a witness to all the noise and mayhem that comes with a polluted mind that won't stay in the moment.

People are constantly dealing with their thoughts that focus on "getting" and "having" and "becoming." We are attached to owning something or attached to becoming something.

When things are not going as planned, your mind flips into worry mode. Worry is always grounded in the fear of the future. Worrisome thoughts are thoughts we give permission to take control of our state of mind. We worry when we lack trust or faith.

If faith is the belief that things will work out, worry is the belief that everything is in danger of falling apart. It won't work out. You could fail. This could happen or that could happen. Your thoughts start to play out the worst-case scenarios of a bad outcome that results in you ending up empty handed, broke, or alone.

Worry is a broken loop of fear. This is a daily struggle with the mind. You want to trust in something bigger than yourself, but you can't. So, how can you fight back against the loop of fear that worry creates? How do you stop worrying about the future "possibilities" and start living?

You'll need to bring yourself back to the present moment. It starts with reframing your situation and life in a positive framework. Are you seeing the world as a scary, frightful place? Are you afraid of waking up and finding yourself homeless one day? Do you think you'll lose your job next week?

Well, all these things could happen—or none of them could happen. The extent to which they happen is up to you. Most of the worst things that will ever happen to you take place in your mind first... and that's it! Think about the grand symphony of chaos that is constantly conducted inside your mind. But you, as the conductor of your thoughts, can choose how and what to think about. Imagine that. You are the master of your own mind. Remind yourself of this fact and take time to observe your thoughts.

We always have ideas, voices and opinions, mixed with conflicting thoughts based on information we are not entirely sure is correct. How do you separate the good from the bad? How can you trust what is real and what is misleading? How do you stay mindful when your mind wants to wander, explore, and create its own reality without permission?

The strategy I use to filter out the thoughts I don't need is a mental discipline that gets you to focus in on just the present moment. As most of your thoughts jump around and can be in the past one minute and the present the next, this form of mental conditioning—also known as **reframing your thinking portal**—works because it turns down the volume on noisy, intrusive thoughts.

Worry is conditioning your thoughts to fear. If you were raised by fearful parents, and spent most of your youth surrounded by fearful people, then being a worrier will seem the best course of action. This way, you build up your fears of the future and don't take any action for fear of failing.

Right now, make a list of three areas of your life you consistently worry about. Knowing what your triggers are plays a big part in this. Then, when you think about these areas, what thoughts enter your mind? Common themes are thoughts of scarcity, losing something valuable, failing fast, or being embarrassed if your master plan doesn't work out.

You might have fearful thoughts of money or relationships, worry about losing your job or getting ill. These are all legitimate worries. But worry leads to mental paralysis by default, and without taking positive action, you'll end up doing nothing. This ensures the worry habit sticks with its rotation and sets up a loop to capture your thoughts. You must unravel that loop and dismantle the worry habit.

You can empower your thoughts by feeding empowering messages to your mind. It works like the body. If you eat crap and junk food, you're going to feel like a physical garbage can. The mind is no different. Worrisome thoughts generate anxiety. You only get out of it what you feed into it.

Here is how you can eliminate the worry habit right now and gain control over the triggers that set you off.

WORRY THOUGHTS ARE FABRICATIONS

Worry is believing in false stories that have not come true. You worry about having no money, and yet, there is no evidence to suggest you will always be broke. Maybe you worry about your health and that you might get sick. Well, you will not be healthy forever, you know that. But you have your health today, don't you? Worrisome thoughts are grounded in future fear, like most things we stress about.

Worry is another form of fear. We create most of our fears. They play out in our minds and take over all common sense. What are you worrying about right now? Is it something now or something supposed to happen later?

When you feed into the worry habit, you reinforce the false stories that will likely never happen.

From now on, feed your mind the good stuff it really wants. Try these affirmations instead:

- "I am not worried about tomorrow because today is perfect. The here and now is what I have."

- "I always worry about losing my job, but this has never happened to me. I am a good employee and the company I work for values its workers. Why would I think it could happen now?"

Break down your worrisome thoughts and expose these demons for what they are: False fabrications that rarely happen. Worry is a habit, and you can break any habit. But you can make your worrisome beliefs come true, too. If you believe that you will be broke, lose your health, or get divorced, then by carrying this worry around with you can manifest it to come true.

Remember: Thoughts have power and can draw toward you the bad as well as the good. If you think you're going to lose your job, you might show up at work acting like someone who doesn't deserve to be there.

Do you think your spouse is going to divorce you? This worry could cause you to become paranoid. Soon you start to track his or her whereabouts until they catch you planting a GPS unit underneath the car. So, while worrisome thinking is grounded in fantasy, you can manifest your worst nightmares to happen by holding onto these worrisome thoughts.

Negative Thinking: Hardwired for Fear

Positive thinking only works if you truly believe the message you're sending to your brain.

There are a few things I want to say about negative thinking. We tend to see negative thinking as something bad that you should be ashamed of. I'll admit that thinking positively and acting in a positive manner is much better than doing things in a negative way. But, it's a philosophy of mine that negative energy is just as important as positive energy.

How can that be?

You must walk through a mile of slimy mud sometimes before you can get to the green grass on the other end. In other words, being negative and experiencing the suffering that goes with it can be a great motivator for making the decision to change.

Negative thinking—or, "living a negative lifestyle", as I like to call it—is a sign that something is not right with your life.

Believe it or not, some people seem to enjoy the attention they receive from negative thinking.

If you have an NMA (i.e., Negative Mental Attitude), and you are not happy with this, deciding to switch over to a positive frame of mind requires that you take intentional action to get your momentum moving.

Some of the world's greatest success stories have come from people who lived through hell and decided to change their lives. You can also look at the people who have everything going for them, and yet, they are unhappy, and it shows in their attitude.

I truly believe that living a positive lifestyle has very little to do with how much you own or how successful you are. It comes down to attitude in every aspect of your life. If all it took was money and popularity, then there wouldn't be any misery with people who seemingly have everything.

Thought and Circumstances: How to Attract What You Want

If you are unhappy with your present circumstances, whether it be your job, relationships, or current state of mind, there is only one way to change it: Think differently. I know this sounds like an obvious piece of advice, but there are reasons for this.

Do you know what happens when you think differently? Things on the outside begin to change. Your situation can only change if you do. Here is why.

Your outer world will always reflect the inner. Your success or failure is based on the success and failure going on inside.

Succeed in programming your thoughts for having positive experiences and that is what will happen.

People have been known to alter the course of their lives with a shift in attitude. Can you imagine where you would be if you focused everything you had on thinking with a positive attitude? This isn't to say thinking alone will change you, but without it, we can't follow up with positive actions.

What exactly are positive actions? Some examples are: helping people, working toward goals that get you unstuck, streamlining your efforts to make life worth living for yourself and those around.

The circumstances of this life do not control you. While we can't always choose our circumstances, we can decide how to view them. It is just a matter of fact that bad things happen. Life doesn't go according to plan, and it isn't always fun—no matter who you are or how positive your thoughts may be. But you can train yourself in the best way to deal with it.

Empower Your Focus (Bonus Chapter #2)

Turn the page to read a chapter from **Empower Your Focus** (Book #4 in the *Pathways to Mastery* series)

The Process of Building Focus

You've understood what focus truly is, why it matters, and how to channel the different forms of focus to your advantage. But how do you go about building focus? Where do you begin? What process do you follow, and how do you ensure your pursuit of building focus is not only fruitful but, is also sustainable and enjoyable?

The key is to begin with one thing to focus on, to complete this task or meet this goal, and then move on to your next pursuit, thus creating a continuous flow of victories, each one fueling the next. Success begets success, and the more wins you rack up, the greater confidence you will develop in your deep focus sessions.

Focus on One Thing Until Done

We've found ourselves in a world where multi-tasking is the norm and focusing on one thing at a time is an exception. However, in doing so, we sacrifice the potential for our brains to level up and cultivate the right mind with the best training.

Conditioning the mind to focus on and accomplish task after task, goal after goal, with the help of the right habits, delivers the outcome you truly desire. Instead of ending up with whatever cheap pleasure that's derived from instant gratification, you reap the benefits of a focused mind trained to execute on priority tasks.

The more we repeatedly do something, the easier it becomes to do; it becomes a pattern, a *good habit*. The scientific term for this practice is 'automaticity'. It's the ability of your mind to let you do something on autopilot. It takes a great deal of effort and time to set up a new habit.

While some studies claim it takes 21 days, others state it takes 66 days and some even say it takes 254 days for a new habit to be fully ingrained in you - but once you've managed to establish a new habit, your activity will be almost automatic. When you focus on one thing only, and one thing after another at a time, each one becomes easier to do as it becomes habitual.

Here are a few techniques which will set you on the path to building focus and sharpening your mind.

Technique 1: Create goals for yourself

It is said that the difference between a dream and a goal is that a dream is a gift you *wish to receive*, whereas a goal is an outcome you *work to achieve*. Without a concrete goal, you can't have a clear plan. Without a plan, your actions will have no particular direction, and your energies will be expended wastefully.

Here are 11 steps to help you identify, articulate, and clearly define your goals:

1. Begin with an idea dump. List out all the things you've wanted to achieve, without setting any limitations in your mind.

2. Choose your master goal. What is it that you want the most in your life? Don't winnow it down – be bold in what you're asking of yourself, and trust that you will figure out a way to make it happen. Once you've chosen your master goal, write it down and commit to it.

3. Put a timeline to your goal. It doesn't matter if it is 2 months, 2 years, or 20 years – but put a definite timeline.

4. Break down your big goal. What will you need to accomplish in the next 1 year? Reverse engineer your big goal by writing down all the steps necessary to achieve it (hence, the next step).

5. Break your big goal down into 'sub-goals'. Make a list of every task, no matter how small, and identify what it is and how much time required to finish it. Think of this as your to-do list – what simple tasks will help you move towards accomplishing your goal?

6. Prioritize your action steps. What do you need to do right away, and what's not as urgent?

7. Visualize your success daily. Feeling how you would feel once you've accomplished your goal will fuel you to work towards it.

8. Become part of a supportive community. Invite accountability into your lifestyle. You don't have to do everything all by yourself!

9. Be mindful of your obstacles. Are you missing key resources? Do you hold limiting beliefs that are sabotaging you in your quest? Be honest and list out your obstacles so that you can find ways to overcome them.

10. Identify the skills and knowledge you need to reach your goal.

11. Continuously and honestly review your progress. Set up weekly and monthly review sessions to get an accurate benchmark of your progress.

Follow these steps and you should be well on your way to building an extraordinary level of focus.

Technique 2: Build 'focus blocks' to improve productivity

Using 'focus blocks' refers to chalking out chunks of time on your calendar for specific activities. Doing your taxes? Block out time on your calendar. Brainstorming ideas for your next project? Set aside time. Whatever task is pressing, whether it be attending your child's concert or much-required me-time, you want to dedicate time exclusively to that activity for that particular period of time.

Scheduling time is the easy part – the harder part is to ensure that you work only on that specific activity for that chunk of time, ignoring all else. This includes not checking up on interrupting emails and not pausing for a colleague dropping by for some quick help.

Here are **7 quick tips** to help you:

1. Commit to your scheduling system.

2. Use your calendar, use your stickies, use a daily planner - use every tool at your disposal to help you stick to your system.

3. Make a reasonable schedule – you don't want to burn out in the process of reaching for your optimum level of focus.

4. Get your colleagues onboard – you can share your calendar so that they can see when you're available.

5. Find a quiet and comfortable spot to work without distraction.

6. Work in sync with your natural cycle. When do you concentrate best? Set your schedule accordingly.

7. Don't give up. If you find yourself off course, gently bring yourself back to plan.

It's hard to get into the system of working with focus blocks. But, once you commit to it—and discuss it with your colleagues—you can request that they not interrupt, and you'll find a tremendous boost in productivity.

Technique 3: Use focus-building activities in a group setting

While the first two techniques were inward-focused, here's another technique to help you start building better focus, and this one can be group-based. Pick a focus-building activity, and schedule time with friends or family centered around this activity. Think 'puzzle-night'!

You probably worked on a lot of puzzles as a child –puzzles are a great way to stimulate the mind and build focus not only in children, but also in adults.

Here are **five benefits** of using puzzles as a work-out for your brain:

1. Improve cognitive function and spatial reasoning

2. Develop better attention to detail

3. Improve your memory, especially short-term memory

4. Enhance your problem-solving ability and IQ over time

5. Immerse yourself in an esteem-boosting activity and reduce stress

If jigsaw puzzles aren't your thing, you can go with crossword games, solve brain teasers, work with Sudoku, or even use apps such as Luminosity. If you're a chess player, it can be a fantastic way improve focus as well.

No matter which technique you choose to begin your journey of improving your ability to focus, you want to ensure you commit to one thing at a time and stay on course.

The process of building focus is an ongoing challenge, but it comes with life-changing rewards that make it totally worth the commitment.

About Scott Allan

Scott Allan is an international bestselling author of over 30 books published in 12 languages in the area of personal growth and self-development. He is the author of **Fail Big, Undefeated,** and **Do the Hard Things First**.

As a former corporate business trainer in Japan, and **Transformational Mindset Strategist**, Scott has invested over 10,000 hours of research and instructional coaching into the areas of self-mastery and leadership training.

With an unrelenting passion for teaching, building critical life skills, and inspiring people around the world to take charge of their lives, Scott Allan is committed to a path of **constant and never-ending self-improvement**.

Many of the success strategies and self-empowerment material that is reinventing lives around the world evolves from Scott Allan's 20 years of practice and teaching critical skills to corporate executives, individuals, and business owners.

You can connect with Scott at:

scottallan@scottallanpublishing.com

www.scottallanpublishing.com

www.scottallanbooks.com

SCOTT ALLAN

"Master Your Life One Book at a Time."

Subscribe to the weekly newsletter for actionable content and updates on future book releases from Scott Allan.

Made in United States
Orlando, FL
06 March 2024